BEFORE IT'S TOO LATE

1000 Spiritual Questions to Ask Myself Before I Die

BEFORE IT'S TOO LATE

1000 Spiritual Questions
to Ask Myself Before
I Die

Self-Reflection for a Peaceful, Purposeful Life and Lasting Legacy

Authors:
Aria Capril Publishing Group
Mauricio Vasquez
First Printing: January 2024

ISBN 978-1-998729-04-3   Electronic book
ISBN 978-1-998729-03-6   Hardcover book
ISBN 978-1-998729-02-9   Paperback

INTRODUCTION

Questions are the essence of our humanity. They drive our curiosity, fuel our growth, and deepen our understanding of ourselves and the world around us. When it comes to contemplating life and death, the power of a well-posed question becomes even more profound. "BEFORE IT'S TOO LATE 1000 Spiritual Questions to Ask Myself Before I Die" is designed to guide you through this deeply personal journey of self-discovery, reflection, and preparation for the final chapters of your life.

Why Are Powerful Questions Essential for Understanding Life and Death?

At the core of this exploration lies the desire to live a life of intention and leave a meaningful legacy. By asking the right questions, you gain clarity about who you are, what you value, and how you wish to be remembered. These questions help you delve into your deepest fears, unearth your most cherished dreams, and align your actions with your true self.

In the whirlwind of everyday life, moments of profound introspection are rare. This book offers you a sanctuary—a structured pathway to pause, reflect, and engage with the most significant aspects of your existence. Each question is crafted to provoke deep thought, inspire emotional healing, and foster spiritual fulfillment, ensuring that your final days are spent with peace, purpose, and profound understanding.

The Importance of Asking the Right Questions

Imagine navigating the end of your life without having truly understood your own desires, fears, and aspirations. The consequences of such a journey can lead to unresolved regrets, strained relationships, and a lingering sense of unfulfillment. By thoughtfully engaging with these 1000 questions, you empower yourself to confront these challenges head-on, transforming potential anxieties into opportunities for growth and acceptance.

What if you uncover aspects of yourself that you had long ignored or misunderstood? What if these questions help you reconcile past regrets, mend broken relationships, or solidify your spiritual beliefs? The journey you embark on with this book is not just about preparing for death—it's about enriching the quality of your remaining days and ensuring that you leave behind a legacy that truly reflects your essence.

Crafting Your Own Path Through Questions

While this book provides a comprehensive set of questions, it also encourages you to create your own personalized inquiries. This flexibility allows you to address specific areas of your life that are uniquely significant to you. Whether you're grappling with existential dilemmas, seeking emotional healing, or planning your legacy, these guidelines will help you formulate questions that resonate deeply with your personal journey.

A Relevant Thought to Guide You

"The unexamined life is not worth living." — Socrates

This timeless wisdom underscores the importance of introspection and self-awareness. By engaging with the questions in this book, you honor this philosophy, ensuring that your life is examined with intention and depth.
Maximizing Your Reflective Journey

There is no need to struggle with finding the right questions or spending endless hours in contemplation. This book has meticulously curated these questions to facilitate a seamless and meaningful reflection process. Each question serves as a catalyst for deeper insight, guiding you toward a harmonious and fulfilled conclusion to your life's journey.

Empower Your Connections:
Discover More Tools to Strengthen Relationships.
Scan the QR Code Today

A NOTE OF GRATITUDE

Dear Reader,

Thank you for choosing "BEFORE IT'S TOO LATE 1000 Spiritual Questions to Ask Myself Before I Die". Your commitment to self-discovery and preparation is a testament to your courage and wisdom. As you embark on this sacred journey, I encourage you to embrace each question with an open heart and a reflective mind.

If this book has touched your life, I kindly ask you to leave a review. Your feedback not only supports my work but also helps others find the guidance and peace they seek. To leave your review, please scan the QR code provided.

Your support means the world to me. Thank you in advance for your help and for being a part of this meaningful journey.

With heartfelt gratitude,

Mauricio

GUIDELINES FOR ASKING PROFOUND QUESTIONS

Embarking on the journey of contemplating life and death requires sensitivity, introspection, and intentional engagement. The following guidelines will help you ask profound questions that unlock deep self-discovery, foster emotional healing, and facilitate meaningful preparation for the final chapters of your life.

1. Embrace Open-Ended Questions for Deep Reflection

Choose open-ended questions that encourage extensive contemplation. These questions should go beyond simple yes or no answers, inviting you to explore the depths of your beliefs, values, and experiences.

2. Focus on Personal Growth and Understanding

Design questions that help you uncover and understand your innermost needs, fears, and desires related to your life and its conclusion. Aim to gain clarity on what truly matters to you as you navigate the end of your journey.

3. Encourage Authentic and Honest Responses

Frame your questions in a way that promotes genuine and sincere answers. Create a safe mental space where you can express your true feelings and thoughts without fear of judgment or reprisal.

4. Prioritize Self-Benefit and Personal Well-Being

Focus on questions that contribute to your personal growth, emotional well-being, and preparation for the end of life. Use these inquiries to enhance your understanding of your life's impact and to foster peace with your past.

5. Delve into Emotional Depths and Healing

Incorporate questions that prompt you to identify, understand, and articulate your emotions regarding mortality and your life. Explore your feelings about fear, hope, and inner calm to navigate the complex emotional landscape associated with approaching death.

6. Shift Focus from Challenges to Opportunities for Growth

When addressing difficult topics such as regrets or unresolved relationships, frame your questions to explore potential resolutions and positive outcomes. Encourage yourself to find ways to achieve emotional peace and mend strained relationships.

7. Maintain a Non-Judgmental and Supportive Tone

Formulate your questions in a neutral and compassionate manner to avoid triggering defensive reactions. Avoid accusatory language or leading phrasing that may hinder honest introspection.

8. Avoid Leading and Biased Questions

Ensure that your questions are unbiased and open-ended, allowing your genuine thoughts and feelings to surface without external influence. This maintains the integrity of your self-discovery process.

9. Keep Questions Clear, Concise, and Focused

Craft questions that are straightforward and easy to understand, avoiding unnecessary complexity that might obscure their intent. Simple questions often lead directly to the core of your reflections.

10. Use Questions as Gateways for Deeper Exploration

Treat each question as a starting point for further reflection. After answering, consider the underlying reasons and broader implications of your response to uncover deeper insights.

TIPS FOR THE USE OF THIS BOOK

"Before It's Too Late: 111 Questions to Ask Myself Before I Die" is more than just a collection of questions—it is a profound tool for self-discovery, reflection, and preparation for the final chapters of your life. To maximize the benefits of this journey, consider the following guidelines:

1. Navigate Through Diverse Dimensions for Comprehensive Reflection

The questions in this book are thoughtfully organized into five key dimensions: Existential and Spiritual Considerations, Emotional and Psychological Concerns, Social and Relational Dimensions, Physical and Medical Factors, and Practical and Logistical Preparations. Each dimension contains numerous subtopics, providing a structured yet flexible framework to explore various aspects of your life and experiences.

2. Embrace Deep Listening to Yourself

The cornerstone of meaningful introspection is active self-listening. Pay attention not only to your thoughts but also to your emotions, physical sensations, and inner energy as you engage with each question.

3. Personalize Your Reflective Process

Tailor the questions to align with your unique life context and current areas of introspection. Feel free to adapt, modify, or rephrase questions to better suit your personal narrative and reflective needs.

4. Engage Creatively and Intuitively

Utilize the open-ended nature of the questions to foster creative and intuitive engagement. Allow your imagination and personal stories to shape your responses.

5. Encourage Follow-Up and Deeper Exploration

Let each answer serve as a gateway to further inquiry and deeper understanding. Use your initial responses as springboards for additional questions and reflections.

6. Maintain Simplicity and Clarity in Your Reflections

Focus on one question at a time to maintain clarity and prevent feeling overwhelmed. Ensure that each question is approached with a clear and open mind.

7. Adapt Questions to Reflect Your Authentic Voice

Modify the questions to align with your personal style and language. This makes the reflection process more natural and engaging for you.

8. Document Your Reflections for Ongoing Insight

Keep a dedicated journal or digital record of your answers. Documenting your reflections allows you to track your emotional and spiritual journey over time.

9. Integrate Questions into Your Daily Routine

Make reflective questioning a consistent part of your daily life. Incorporate questions into your morning or evening routines to provide structure and continuity to your introspection.

10. Share and Discuss Your Insights with Trusted Individuals

Openly share your reflections with trusted friends, family members, or support groups. Discussing your answers can offer new perspectives and deepen your relationships through shared vulnerability.

TABLE OF CONTENTS

Chapter 1. Existential and Spiritual Considerations

1.1.   **Meaning of Life and Legacy**: Reflecting on what one's life has stood for, what lessons have been learned and taught, and how one's actions have contributed to the world.

Below is a set of introspective questions focused on the theme of "Meaning of Life and Legacy". Each category invites you to examine your life experiences, relationships, unrealized aspirations, and the deeper search for meaning that comes to the forefront as you are near the end of life. These questions encourage a profound engagement with your spiritual identity, calling, and sense of destiny, helping you bring clarity, peace, and reconciliation.

a. Personal Experiences and Core Life Lessons

Formative Moments

- What are the pivotal moments in my life—the successes and setbacks—that most shaped who I am today?
- How did I respond to adversity and what strengths did I discover in those challenging times?
- In looking back at all I have experienced, what patterns or themes emerge that define my life's journey?

Values and Principles

- Which personal values guided my decisions, and how consistently did I uphold them?
- How have my beliefs, morals, or guiding principles evolved over time?
- Where did I find my greatest sense of purpose—through family, work, service, creativity, or faith?

Internal Growth and Transformation

- Which personal qualities do I consider my most significant achievements (e.g., compassion, resilience, integrity)?
- How did I learn to overcome fear, doubt, or insecurity, and how did that growth influence my later choices?
- Am I at peace with whom I have become, and if not, what understanding or healing would help me reconcile my inner conflicts?

b. Relationships and Interpersonal Connections

Love and Support

- Who were the most influential people in my life, and how did their presence shape my character and path?
- Whom I have loved most deeply, and how did I express that love in words and actions?
- How did I show gratitude and appreciation to those who supported me or guided me along the way?

Impact on Others

- Whose lives have I touched or influenced in meaningful ways—whether through mentorship, kindness, or simply being present?
- How did I contribute to my community, my culture, or my spiritual tradition, and how might these contributions endure?
- What lessons did I pass on to younger generations, friends, colleagues, or descendants, and do I believe these lessons will help them navigate life?

Reconciliation and Closure

- Are there relationships I wish to mend, apologies I need to make, or forgiveness I need to offer? Why would that be important?
- Did I communicate my appreciation and farewell to the important people in my life? If not, how can I do so now?
- How can I honor the interconnectedness of my life with others, acknowledging both positive and painful relationships with understanding and peace?

c. **Unfulfilled Goals, Unresolved Conflicts, and Life's Limitations**

Unrealized Aspirations

- Which dreams or ambitions remain unfulfilled, and why did these goals go unmet?
- Can I find meaning in letting go of what I didn't achieve, recognizing my human limitations and the richness in what I accomplished instead? How could I do that?
- What insights can I gain from my unfulfilled goals that might help others find acceptance and direction in their own lives?

Regrets and Healing

- Do I carry regrets about actions taken or not taken, words spoken or left unsaid? Why is that?
- What steps can I take—even now—to release feelings of guilt, disappointment, or sorrow?
- How might acknowledging my imperfections and mistakes serve as a lesson in humility, patience, and grace for those I leave behind?

Acceptance of Impermanence

- How do I understand the impermanence of my achievements, possessions, and social roles?
- Can I accept it is natural not to accomplish everything I once intended, and that the measure of a life is more than a list of successes? How could I facilitate such acceptance?
- How might embracing impermanence free me to find deeper meaning in what I have done rather than what I have not?

d. The Search for Meaning, Spiritual Understanding, and Reconciliation

Spiritual Insights and Faith

- How have my spiritual beliefs or religious traditions shaped my understanding of life's purpose and ultimate meaning?
- What wisdom or spiritual truths resonate most deeply as I face the unknown beyond physical life?
- Have my spiritual practices—prayer, meditation, reflection, community worship—brought me closer to understanding my role in the grand tapestry of existence? If not, why might that be?

Alignment with a Higher Purpose

- Did I live in alignment with what I believe to be a higher calling or divine plan? What could be such a higher calling or divine plan for me?
- In what ways did I serve others, contribute to the greater good, or advance causes that uplifted humanity or honored the sacredness of all life?
- Can I recognize my life as part of a larger story, finding meaning in the interplay of my individual journey with the collective human and spiritual narrative? What would be the meaning of my life?

Peace at the Threshold

- As I approach the end of my earthly experience, what truths bring me comfort and clarity about my legacy?
- How can I integrate past joys and sorrows, achievements and failures into a unified understanding that brings peace to my spirit?
- Am I able to surrender to what lies beyond with a sense of trust, hopeful anticipation, or inner calm, knowing I have done my best to live meaningfully? If not, how could I achieve it?

e. Synthesizing the Journey

Summation of a Life Well-Lived

- If I could distill my life's essence into a single message or teaching, what would it be?

- How do I hope others will remember me in terms of my character, my contributions, and the love I shared?
- In acknowledging the totality of my journey, how have my experiences, relationships, successes, and setbacks contributed to a legacy that endures in the hearts and minds of those I've touched?

Guiding Others with My Story

- What guidance would I offer to someone younger or at an earlier stage of life, based on the wisdom I've gained?
- How can my legacy serve as a bridge, connecting my past to others' futures, providing insight and inspiration beyond my own lifespan?

By engaging deeply with these questions, you can more clearly discern the arc of your spiritual vocation—from formative spiritual awakenings, through relationships that nurtured or tested your faith, to unfulfilled goals and tensions that proved instructive. This reflective process enables you to find peace with your spiritual identity, acknowledge your unique contributions, and recognize your role in the grand mosaic of existence. Ultimately, such introspection encourages a gentle and compassionate acceptance of your spiritual destiny, offering comfort, meaning, and a sense of divine accompaniment.

1.2. Spiritual Purpose and Vocation: Contemplating one's spiritual calling, destiny, or role within a greater spiritual framework.

Below is a set of introspective questions centered on "Spiritual Purpose and Vocation". These questions invite deep reflection on how your spiritual calling has been shaped by personal experiences, relationships, unmet aspirations, and the innate search for meaning. Thoughtfully organized into key subcategories, they aim to evoke self-awareness, healing, and spiritual growth as one nears the end of life's journey.

a. Personal Experiences and Memories: Tracing the Arc of a Spiritual Journey

Formative Spiritual Encounters

- Which life events awakened or deepened my sense of spiritual calling—moments of wonder, crisis, or inner realization?
- What moments in my life stand out as times when I felt unmistakably guided by a higher power, guardian presence, or divine inspiration?
- How have my spiritual beliefs evolved over the years, and what turning points or experiences led to these changes?

Embodied Values and Principles

- In what ways did my choices, habits, and actions reflect my spiritual vocation throughout my life?

- How do my professed values compare to the way I've lived each day, and what insights can I gain from any areas of discrepancy?
- Which qualities—compassion, generosity, resilience—were most closely tied to my spiritual identity, and how did I cultivate them?

Interplay of Faith and Struggle

- When confronted with hardship, illness, loss, or doubt, how did my spiritual understanding shift or mature?
- How did I reconcile human suffering and injustice with my belief in a greater spiritual framework?
- How did adversity influence my sense of purpose and faith, and in what ways might it have challenged or deepened my spiritual understanding?

b. Relationships and Interpersonal Connections: Finding Spiritual Purpose Through Others

Mentors, Guides, and Teachers

- Who were the spiritual mentors or role models that helped shape my understanding of purpose and calling?
- How did their examples, teachings, or kindness influence my personal spiritual path?
- In what ways did I honor or pass forward the guidance I received, and how might this have contributed to the continuity of spiritual wisdom within my community or family?

Offering Spiritual Support to Others

- In what ways did I act as a spiritual guide, friend, or confidant, inspiring others to seek truth, compassion, or inner peace?
- In what ways did I listen to and support those who were searching for meaning, and how might I have shown them empathy and understanding?
- How might others remember the spiritual gifts I shared—be they comfort in times of grief, wisdom in times of confusion, or encouragement in moments of doubt?

Reconciling Differences and Finding Unity

- Were there relationships strained by differing beliefs, and how did I attempt to bridge these spiritual divides?
- What perspectives or experiences might help me develop deeper understanding and compassion for those whose paths and convictions differ from my own?
- How can I offer forgiveness and seek reconciliation with those who challenged my spiritual identity, leaving a legacy of healing rather than discord?

c. Unfulfilled Goals, Unresolved Conflicts, and the Complexity of Spiritual Calling

Acknowledging Unmet Aspirations

- What aspects of my spiritual vocation, such as further service, study, pilgrimage, or deeper meditation, did I hope to pursue but have not yet explored?
- How might recognizing that not all spiritual aims need completion within one lifetime bring me peace and affirm the meaning of my sincere efforts?
- How does acknowledging human limitations help me to practice humility and acceptance at this stage of life?

Transforming Regret into Insight

- Which decisions do I wish I could revisit, and can I derive spiritual wisdom from understanding why I made them at the time?
- How might embracing regret as a teacher—rather than a burden—open my heart to greater empathy for myself and others?
- How might I view my unrealized spiritual goals as signposts that guide future generations toward growth and enlightenment, rather than as failures?

Facing Internal Conflict and Doubt

- How have I wrestled with existential questions that remain unanswered, and what helps me accept the mystery that surrounds them?
- How did I grapple with periods of spiritual dryness, skepticism, or anger at the divine or fate?
- How might I reconcile my inner tensions by viewing them as intrinsic to the human condition, and what meaning can I find in the search itself?

d. The Search for Meaning and Reconciliation: Integrating Life's Lessons into a Spiritual Whole

Awareness of a Greater Pattern

- What threads of meaning, purpose, and guidance can I discern as I reflect on my life's journey?
- How might my spiritual calling fit into a larger narrative—one that extends beyond my individual life and touches the universal human spirit?
- How have my contributions, values, and personal growth added something valuable to the world, and what does this reveal about my life's purpose?

Finding Inner Peace and Acceptance

- As I approach the threshold of mortality, how can I embrace what I have accomplished and release what I have not?
- How can I find trust in the divine or the cosmic order to honor my sincere efforts to align with my spiritual calling?
- How does achieving an inner harmony—between action and intention, faith and doubt—help me face the unknown with equanimity?

Guiding Future Generations

- What spiritual insights, stories, or blessings can I leave behind, so that others might discover their own sense of purpose?
- How might my life's lessons serve as seeds that will grow in the hearts and minds of those who come after me?
- How might my legacy inspire compassion, understanding, or deeper reflection in others, extending my spiritual vocation beyond my lifespan?

e. **Embracing the Sacredness of the Journey: Stepping into the Mystery with Grace**

Surrender and Trust

- How can I surrender my life's narrative—its triumphs, struggles, and incomplete chapters—to the divine mystery at its center?
- How does trusting in a greater spiritual framework help me find comfort as I transition beyond this life?
- How can I appreciate the sacredness of this final step, viewing it not as an end, but as a passage that may lead to greater understanding?

Presence and Contemplation

- What final meditations, prayers, or blessings might I offer to myself and those I love?
- What steps can I take to allow each breath to anchor me in the present moment, fostering rest and freedom from judgment or striving?

By engaging with these questions, you gain an opportunity to re-examine your spiritual vocation in its entirety, its roots in personal history, its expression of relationships, its unfulfilled aspirations, and its ultimate meaning. This process encourages peaceful reconciliation with your own self, others, and the divine, illuminating the path toward a dignified and spiritually fulfilling conclusion in life's journey.

1.3. **Connection to the Divine or Sacred: Engaging with God, a higher power, or a universal spirit. Questions of trust, faith, love, mercy, and divine presence.**

Below is a set of questions focused on the theme of "Connection to the Divine or Sacred". These questions invite you to carefully examine your relationship with God, a higher power, or the universal spirit as you near the end of life. Each subcategory guides you through personal memories, relationships, unresolved issues, and the search for meaning, trust, and reconciliation. The aim is to evoke honest introspection, spiritual growth, and peace.

a. **Personal Encounters with the Sacred: Recalling Moments of Divine Presence**

Formative Spiritual Memories

- What moments of awe, gratitude, or profound inner calm have made me feel powerfully connected to the divine?
- How did I experience sacred presence in the ordinary rhythms of life—through nature, music, prayer, or silent reflection?
- Which life events or turning points seemed guided or illuminated by a higher spiritual hand?

Evolving Understanding of the Divine

- How has my understanding of God, a higher power, or spiritual reality changed over time, and what prompted these shifts?
- Were there stages of my life where I felt more distant from the divine, and what did I learn from that perceived absence?
- How have spiritual practices such as prayer, meditation, or ritual deepened my sense of connection, and what impact did they have on my journey?

Interpreting Spiritual Struggles and Triumphs

- When I faced suffering, injustice, or loss, how did these experiences shape my faith or trust in a higher power?
- How have I experienced divine grace or mercy through unexpected outcomes, guidance, or resilience during difficult times?
- What moments of despair have taught me about compassion, empathy, and the sacred mystery of life?

b. **Relationships and Divine Influence: Spiritual Dimensions of Interpersonal Connections**

Expressions of Divine Love Through Others

- In which relationships did I feel divine love—perhaps reflected in kindness, patience, or support from others?

- How have I acted as an instrument of the divine to those around me, providing comfort, wisdom, or encouragement?
- Who are the individuals that strengthened my faith or showed divine mercy or forgiveness through their actions?

Reconciling Differences Through Faith

- How have spiritual teachings inspired me to seek forgiveness, understanding, or reconciliation in strained relationships?
- How did my belief in a higher power influence how I treated others—did it inspire generosity, acceptance, or humility?
- What steps can I take to release grievances or resentments and trust that divine love encompasses all souls, including those who have hurt me?

Shared Sacred Journeys

- How have communal worship, spiritual gatherings, or religious traditions impacted my sense of shared spiritual purpose?
- What did I learn about love, compassion, and unity under the sacred through my participation in faith communities?
- What helps me appreciate the uniqueness of each person's spiritual path and trust that divine guidance is available to everyone in their own way?

c. Unfulfilled Goals, Unresolved Conflicts, and the Quest for Divine Understanding

Confronting Spiritual Shortcomings

- What spiritual aspirations—such as deeper faith, more devout practice, or a greater understanding of sacred teachings—have I longed to achieve but feel remain incomplete?
- How can I find acceptance in acknowledging that my human limitations did not diminish divine love for me?
- What helps me embrace humility in acknowledging that full spiritual enlightenment may not be attained, and how so can I trust that growth continues beyond this life?

Reconciling Inner Conflict

- How have I wrestled with doubts, spiritual dryness, or anger toward the divine, and what steps can I take to release these now, trusting that I did my best to seek truth?
- What helps me forgive myself for moments when I turned away from the sacred or struggled to embody the values I hold dear?
- How might embracing mystery and uncertainty bring me closer to divine presence, instead of viewing uncertainty as spiritual failure?

Finding Peace in Unanswered Prayers

- How have unanswered prayers or pleas shaped my understanding of divine wisdom, and what has helped me reconcile these experiences with my expectations?
- How can I find comfort in trusting that the sacred responds in ways that may remain hidden or subtle to human understanding?
- What allows me to let go of disappointment and find peace in believing that compassion, rather than judgment, underlies the sacred design?

d. The Search for Meaning, Trust, and Reconciliation in the Face of Mortality

Surrendering to the Divine Will

- How can I surrender to a higher order or divine plan, embracing the idea that my life story is part of a larger tapestry of meaning?
- How can trust in divine love help me release fears about what comes after death, allowing faith to soothe my anxiety?
- What reassures me that the essence of my being—my soul or spirit—will remain embraced by divine presence as my physical life ends?

Embodying Sacred Qualities

- Have I learned to embody attributes commonly associated with the divine—compassion, mercy, forgiveness, unconditional love—and how did they shape my life?
- How can I find peace in knowing that striving to reflect divine qualities has been a sacred purpose in itself as I face mortality?
- How do these qualities guide me now, encouraging me to step into the unknown with courage and grace?

Reconciliation with the Sacred Mystery

- What helps me accept the mystery of divine reality without needing all the answers as I approach the end of my journey?
- How does acknowledging my finite understanding enhance my reverence for the infinite, the eternal, and the unseen?
- How so can I trust the divine recognizes and honors my sincere efforts, honest questions, and the love I shared, even with my human imperfections?

e. Integrating Lessons and Embracing Divine Presence in the Final Moments

Celebrating Divine Encounters

- Which memories of feeling deeply loved, guided, or comforted by the divine do I hold closest to my heart now?
- How can recalling these moments of communion with the sacred bring me peace and reassurance as I take my final steps?
- What helps me feel I am not alone and that a loving presence envelops and sustains me as I approach life's end?

Offering Gratitude and Blessing

- How can I express gratitude for the life I've been given, the spiritual insights I've gained, and the love I've shared?
- What blessings can I offer to others, invoking divine grace that transcends my physical presence and endures after I am gone?
- How might I envision my ultimate moments as part of a sacred homecoming, where divine compassion patiently awaits my arrival?

By engaging with these questions, you can journey inward to explore and affirm your connection to the divine. This process helps foster a deeper sense of trust, reconciliation, and spiritual fulfillment, illuminating the path from fear and uncertainty toward a peaceful embrace of love, mercy, and divine presence as life's final chapter unfolds.

1.4. Religious Beliefs and Practices: Reevaluating religious traditions, rituals, prayers, or scriptures that bring solace or clarity at life's end.

Below is a set of introspective questions designed to guide you through a thoughtful reevaluation of your religious beliefs and practices as they approach the end of life. Each subcategory addresses different dimensions—personal experiences, relationships, unfulfilled goals, and the quest for meaning and reconciliation—ensuring that no vital aspect is overlooked. These questions aim to foster deep reflection, personal growth, and spiritual clarity.

a. Personal Experiences and Memories: Tracing the Spiritual Narrative

Formative Encounters with Faith

- Which religious traditions, rituals, or spiritual teachings first resonated with me, and how did they shape my early understanding of faith?
- What ceremonies, prayers, or scriptures have provided me with comfort or insight during challenging times, and how so have they shaped my spiritual journey?
- How has my perception of sacred texts and religious practices evolved throughout my life, and what prompted these changes?

Moments of Clarity and Doubt

- When did my religious beliefs feel most alive and authentic? Were there moments when worship, prayer, or study brought undeniable solace or clarity?
- Conversely, when did I question or struggle with the relevance of certain traditions or doctrines, and what did this inner tension teach me?
- What meaning have I discovered in the fervent seasons of faith and the quieter, more uncertain periods of my spiritual journey?

Embodied Religious Practice

- How have specific rituals—such as fasting, confession, pilgrimage, or communal worship—deepened my faith, and what meaning have they brought to my spiritual journey?
- What have I learned about distinguishing between the external forms of religion—such as rituals and dogmas—and the internal essence of faith, like love, compassion, and transcendence?
- How can I honor both my religious heritage and my personal spiritual evolution, acknowledging that beliefs and practices are not static but living aspects of my life story?

b. ## Relationships and Interpersonal Connections: Faith as a Bridge or Barrier

Shared Spiritual Journeys

- In what ways did I share my religious beliefs with loved ones, children, friends, or a faith community? Did these interactions strengthen mutual understanding or create tension?
- Who are the individuals—parents, mentors, clergy—who guided my religious development, and what enduring lessons have I learned from them?
- How did communal worship, group study, or shared prayer contribute to my sense of belonging and reinforce my religious identity?

Reconciling Differences in Faith

- Were there relationships strained by differing religious convictions or practices, and how did I navigate these differences?
- How can I forgive myself and others for conflicts rooted in religious misunderstandings, dogmatic rigidity, or spiritual pride, and what steps might help me find peace?
- How can I recognize the sincerity and humanity in those whose beliefs diverge from mine, affirming that multiple paths may lead to spiritual truth?

Legacy and Spiritual Influence

- What spiritual seeds have I planted in the lives of those who remain—through teaching, example, or silent witness—and how might these seeds continue to grow?
- As I approach life's end, how can I acknowledge and celebrate the ways in which my faith, however imperfect, helped shape a more compassionate and ethical community?
- How can I trust that my legacy of belief and practice, even if not fully realized, will provide future generations with points of reflection and inspiration?

c. Unfulfilled Goals and Unresolved Conflicts: Seeking Resolution in Religious Context

Unrealized Aspirations of Faith

- What religious endeavors—such as deep scriptural study, pilgrimages, advanced theological learning, or leadership within my faith tradition—did I intend to pursue but never fulfill, and how so do they remain meaningful to me?
- How can I find peace with the spiritual aspirations that remained out of reach, trusting that sincerity of effort holds value even without final completion?
- How can I trust that divine compassion or grace recognizes the sincerity of my efforts, even when the outcomes were not measurable?

Moral and Ethical Shortcomings

- What instances of harmful words, actions, or neglect might reveal ways I failed to embody my religious values, and how can I address any lingering regret or shame?
- How can I seek forgiveness through prayer, confession, or quiet reflection, and what steps might help me release these burdens while trusting in divine mercy?
- How might embracing humility and contrition, rather than self-judgment, bring about spiritual healing and reconciliation?

Tensions Between Tradition and Inner Truth

- What religious customs did I feel compelled to follow despite them not aligning with my conscience, and how so can I reconcile that tension as I approach the end of life?

- How can I reconcile evolving spiritual understanding with inherited doctrines, and what helps me find reverence in the tradition that nurtured me despite these conflicts?
- How can I make peace with unresolved questions, trusting that it is natural for faith to transcend neat conclusions?

d. **The Search for Meaning and Reconciliation: Integrating Past and Present Faith Experiences**

Finding Solace in Ritual and Scripture

- Which prayers, hymns, or passages of sacred text bring me comfort now, addressing my fears, uncertainties, and hopes at life's threshold?
- How can I reinterpret or rediscover familiar religious symbols, stories, or teachings so they resonate more profoundly during these last days?
- How can I use spiritual disciplines—such as meditation, chanting, or recitation—to invite calmness, acceptance, and divine presence into this sacred time?

Embracing the Core Essence of Faith

- Beyond doctrines and ritual forms, what core truth lies at the heart of my religious tradition—love, service, justice, forgiveness—and how can I anchor myself in this essence now?
- What common moral and spiritual values do I see across religions, and how so can this broadened perspective foster greater understanding and unity in my final reflections?
- How does reconnecting with the spiritual foundation of my faith help me approach death with dignity, grace, and peace?

Trust, Meaning, and Transcendence

- How can I nurture trust in divine compassion, eternal wisdom, or universal love as I prepare to leave this earthly existence behind?
- How might my religious beliefs provide a lens through which to view death not as an ending, but as a passage or transition into a deeper spiritual reality?
- How can accepting the limitations of human understanding bring me comfort in the mystery that envelops all existence, and what helps me trust that the source of life honors my journey?

e. **Integrating the Journey: Accepting a Faithful Legacy**

Consolidating Faith Experiences

- What ways have my religious beliefs and practices shaped my identity, guided my decisions, and provided solace during times of pain as I reflect on my life?
- How can I weave together the fragments of my spiritual journey—moments of devotion, doubt, celebration, and lament—into a coherent and meaningful tapestry of faith?

Offering Gratitude and Letting Go

- What allows me to express gratitude for the spiritual traditions and communities that nurtured me, even as I acknowledge their human imperfections?
- How can gratitude for these guiding influences help me let go of resentment, disappointment, or confusion, clearing space for peace and contentment?

Embracing the Sacred Transition

- How can I envision this final stage of life as a sacred rite of passage, supported by the prayers, blessings, and wisdom that have guided me on my journey?
- How might I carry forward the essence of my beliefs—trust, love, humility—into whatever reality lies beyond the veil of death?

By engaging with these questions, you can gain deeper insight into your spiritual heritage, reconcile lingering tensions, and draw comfort from the wellsprings of religious faith. In this profound examination, the soul finds the courage to embrace transition, guided by teachings, rituals, and divine presence that have shaped and supported you throughout your life's journey.

1.5. Rituals of Transition: Considering ceremonies that honor the soul's journey, from final blessings to anointing rites, aiding a peaceful passage.

Below is a set of reflective and introspective questions centered on "Rituals of Transition"—ceremonies, blessings, anointings, and other sacred practices that honor the soul's journey at life's end. These questions are arranged into meaningful subcategories that address personal experiences, relationships, unresolved matters, and the search for meaning. They are intended to guide you in discovering which rituals resonate most deeply, encourage peace, and support spiritual growth as you prepare for your final transition.

a. Personal Experiences and Memories: Revisiting the Roots of Ritual

Reflecting on Past Rituals and Ceremonies

- Which religious or cultural ceremonies have I experienced in my life (weddings, baptisms, funerals) that left a lasting spiritual impression?
- Were there specific rites—lighting candles, chanting prayers, receiving blessings—that brought me comfort or a sense of connection to something greater?
- What rituals brought me reassurance or healing during times of crisis, grief, or transition, and how so did these ceremonies hold such meaning for me?

Honoring Life's Milestones Through Ritual

- What moments in my life were marked by rituals that helped me transition from one stage or identity to another, and how so did these experiences shape me?
- How did these past ceremonies shape my understanding of the sacredness of beginnings and endings?
- What personal traditions or symbolic acts—such as journaling, visiting a sacred place, or reciting a prayer—have I used to navigate life's changes, and how do they continue to hold power for me at this time?

Personal Preferences and Comfort Zones

- What draws me more deeply—formal, structured rituals rooted in a faith tradition, or simple, personalized gestures that feel intimate and authentic—and how so have these practices shaped my spiritual experience?
- How important is it that my final rituals reflect my cultural or familial heritage, and why?
- As I approach death, what elements—music, silence, incense, scripture, nature—might best create an atmosphere of peace and acceptance?

b. Relationships and Interpersonal Connections: Rituals as Bridges of Love and Understanding

Including Loved Ones in the Ritual Process

- What role do I envision my closest family members, friends, or spiritual leaders playing in my final ceremonies or blessings?

- What gestures—such as holding hands, sharing stories, or reading prayers—might strengthen bonds and provide comfort to both my loved ones and myself?
- How can I express gratitude, love, and forgiveness through a ritual setting that encourages open-hearted sharing?

Community and Collective Spiritual Support

- How might a communal vigil, chanting circle, or final prayer service ease the sense of isolation that can come with dying and affirm my place within a supportive community?
- What religious rites from my tradition emphasize interconnection and solidarity, and how so do they reassure everyone that our spirits remain intertwined?
- How might inviting a spiritual mentor, chaplain, or faith leader to perform certain rites help guide both me and my loved ones through this sacred threshold?

Reconciliation and Letting Go

- How might rituals such as anointing with oil, offering symbolic gifts, or reciting forgiveness prayers help heal old wounds before I depart?
- Which ceremonies encourage dialogue, enabling me to speak openly and receive acceptance, understanding, or pardon from those I leave behind?
- How might a structured farewell ritual help release lingering resentments, regrets, or misunderstandings, allowing all parties to find peace?

c. **Unfulfilled Goals, Unresolved Conflicts, and Ritual as a Path to Closure**

Addressing Unfinished Spiritual Aspirations

- What spiritual practices or ceremonies—such as pilgrimages, blessings, vows, or dedications—have I always intended to explore, and how might I now symbolically acknowledge them as I prepare for the end?
- How might I adapt a familiar rite to symbolize my readiness to surrender unaccomplished dreams or unfulfilled spiritual endeavors into divine or universal care?
- How might performing or planning a final ritual affirm that my efforts and intentions still carry value, even if not fully realized?

Healing Inner Friction Through Ritual

- What kind of ritual might help me confront, express, and release struggles with religious doubts, anger toward the divine, or uncertainty about my faith?

- What kind of ceremony could symbolize my letting go of expectations, fears, or past spiritual failures, and how might it help me embrace peace and forgiveness?
- How might a ritual of acknowledgement—lighting a candle for each regret, writing an apology or prayer—transform unresolved conflicts into seeds of spiritual understanding?

Ritualizing Farewells to Unmet Desires

- What simple, meaningful act—such as casting flowers into a stream or offering a prayer at dawn—might represent the release of my unfinished plans and help me trust that they have served their purpose?
- What tangible symbols—such as letters, objects, or artwork—might I incorporate into a rite to say a final goodbye and lay my burdens down?
- How does ritual help me accept limitations, recognizing that what I leave undone may inspire or instruct others who continue life's journey?

d. The Search for Meaning, Reconciliation, and Spiritual Growth: Embracing the Sacred Threshold

Anchoring in Transcendent Truths

- Which rituals—from my faith tradition or personal spiritual repertoire—affirm that life does not end at physical death, but transitions into a new realm or state of being?
- How might a ceremony of blessing, anointing, or final prayer deepen my trust in a higher power or universal spirit as I navigate this passage?
- How might performing a ritual that evokes ancient wisdom, sacred texts, or timeless practices connect me to a continuum of souls who have crossed this threshold before?

Cultivating Inner Peace and Acceptance

- What rites of surrender—such as a prayer of release, a final chant, or a quiet vigil—might help me accept my mortality with courage and serenity?
- How can ritual help me acknowledge the beauty and meaning of my life's journey, even as I relinquish my hold on this world?
- Which ceremonies can best remind me that I am held in love, grace, and mercy, offering solace in the face of uncertainty?

Transcending Boundaries and Finding Unity

- What kind of ritual that merges elements from different traditions might reflect the universal nature of this human passage and reaffirm our shared spiritual destiny?

- How does participating in a sacred rite expand my perspective, allowing me to see my life as part of a larger cosmic tapestry rather than an isolated event?
- How might a final ritual gently remind me that, in passing, I remain connected to the living, the departed, and the divine source that animates all existence?

e.   Integrating the Ritual Experience into the Final Moments

Selecting or Creating Meaningful Rituals

- Based on all my reflections, which specific ceremonies, rites, or symbolic acts feel most aligned with my beliefs, values, and emotional needs?
- How might discussing these ritual choices openly with loved ones or spiritual advisors ensure that my wishes are honored and understood?
- What guidance—such as written instructions, recorded prayers, or chosen readings—can I leave for others to carry out these rituals on my behalf if I am no longer able?

Embodying the Ritual Spirit in Daily Living

- How can I begin incorporating small, sacred acts now—blessing my meals, lighting a candle at dusk, offering silent prayers of gratitude—so that my life's final stage is already imbued with reverence and intention?
- How does practicing these rituals remind me that my transition is not an abrupt end, but the culmination of a life lived consciously and spiritually?

Trusting in the Sacred Journey

- How can I trust that these rituals hold meaning beyond my immediate understanding, offering spiritual support and guidance as I prepare to step beyond the physical world?
- How does knowing that I can shape my final transition through ritual empower me to face death not with fear, but with a quiet assurance that I am part of a sacred unfolding?

By contemplating these questions, you can thoughtfully approach the selection, adaptation, or creation of end-of-life rituals. This reflective process ensures that your final ceremonies will resonate authentically, promote healing and understanding, and ultimately guide your soul toward a peaceful, spiritually enriched passage.

1.6.   Afterlife and Continuity of Consciousness: Contemplating what follows physical death—heaven, reincarnation, spiritual realms, or the unknown.

Below is a set of reflective and introspective questions designed to guide you in contemplating the afterlife and continuity of consciousness as you approach the end of life. The questions are grouped into meaningful subcategories, each addressing personal memories, relationships, unresolved issues, and the search for meaning. They aim to inspire you through deep spiritual growth, honest self-examination, and a sense of peace in the face of the unknown.

a. **Personal Experiences and Memories: Tracing Clues of a Greater Reality**

Moments of Transcendence

- What times in my life have I sensed a presence or reality beyond the material world—feeling guided, protected, or deeply connected to something infinite?
- What dreams, visions, or coincidences have I experienced that seemed to hint at life's continuity beyond physical boundaries?
- When I encountered loss or near-death experiences, did I gain insights that reshaped my understanding of what happens after we pass?

Spiritual Influences on Beliefs

- Which spiritual traditions, religious teachings, or philosophical perspectives shaped my earliest understanding of an afterlife or spiritual realm?
- How have my beliefs evolved—have I become more certain, more questioning, or more open to multiple possibilities as I've aged?
- What meaningful life lessons or moral values have I discovered that feel too profound to be confined to a single lifetime?

Attunement to the Inner Self

- What aspects of my inner life—conscience, intuition, empathy—suggest that my being extends beyond physical existence?
- What practices, such as meditation, prayer, or contemplation, have I developed that connect me to a sense of eternity or timelessness?
- What qualities within me—such as love, creativity, or compassion—feel as if they could persist beyond physical form?

b. **Relationships and Interpersonal Connections: Eternal Bonds and Shared Destinies**

Love and Continuity

- How does the depth of love I share with certain individuals suggest that our bond might transcend physical life?

- How can I imagine my relationships continuing or transforming in another realm—through memory, energy, or spiritual presence—beyond death?
- How do stories, traditions, and cultural beliefs about reuniting with loved ones after death resonate with my heart and instincts?

Spiritual Guidance and Support

- What influence might ancestors, guides, or spiritual teachers who have passed on have on my journey, and how have I experienced their presence?
- How might my compassion, encouragement, or wisdom continue to reach and uplift those I leave behind, even beyond my physical absence?
- How does picturing my loved ones and me as eternal souls, interconnected and evolving together, bring comfort and ease fear at this threshold?

Healing and Forgiveness Across Boundaries

- How might believing that consciousness endures help me extend forgiveness or seek understanding from those no longer alive, trusting in a divine or cosmic harmony?
- How might acknowledging the possibility of future encounters or connections with departed souls inspire me to resolve conflicts and mend emotional wounds in the present?
- How does envisioning an afterlife soften regrets, allowing me to release resentment and accept that true reconciliation might still be possible beyond this earthly plane?

c. **Unfulfilled Goals, Unresolved Conflicts, and the Notion of Growth Beyond Death**

Transcending Incompleteness

- How might the idea of reincarnation, spiritual progression, or evolving consciousness help me accept that my soul's learning may not be finished at death's door?
- What ambitions, gifts, or lessons did I not fully realize in this life, and how might imagining growth continuing in another form of existence bring me comfort?
- How might viewing life's unfinished projects and relationships as part of a larger tapestry help me release anxiety about leaving them undone?

Eternal Justice and Understanding

- How does belief in a spiritual continuum where truth, balance, or karmic justice prevails bring solace when human fairness falls short?

- How might trusting that the soul's journey includes stages beyond mortality help me reconcile pain, adversity, and unanswered questions?
- What broader context does the idea of an afterlife provide in which all lives, including my own, might find ultimate purpose and resolution?

Embracing the Unknown with Courage

- How can I approach the mysteries surrounding death's aftermath as opportunities for spiritual growth rather than as endpoints?
- What helps me find peace in the notion that what remains unclear now might become clearer in another dimension of consciousness?
- How does considering an eternal perspective help me let go of regret, fear, and striving, replacing them with acceptance and trust?

d. **The Search for Meaning, Reconciliation, and Spiritual Peace: Embracing the Mystery**

Rooting in Faith and Philosophy

- Which concepts—heavenly realms, unity with the divine, collective consciousness—resonate most, and why do they bring me comfort?
- What scriptures, spiritual texts, or philosophical works have I read that illuminate the afterlife, and how do they inspire calm and hope?
- How might integrating insights from various traditions—religious, mystical, and scientific—broaden my understanding of life's continuity?

Aligning Morality and Purpose

- How does believing in a continuity of consciousness influence my values, guiding me to live with greater kindness, honesty, and generosity here and now?
- How does the possibility of an afterlife encourage me to view death not as an end, but as a meaningful transition within a larger cosmic narrative?
- What helps me let go of fear and embrace death as a sacred crossing, trusting in a divine order or universal intelligence to guide me beyond the veil?

Surrender and Ultimate Reconciliation

- How might accepting the unknown bring a new kind of freedom, allowing me to let go of rigid expectations and surrender to the mystery of what lies ahead?
- What steps can I take to release intellectual certainties and trust in an ineffable truth that may only be fully understood after passing through death's door?
- How might I reconcile myself to this uncertain future by acknowledging that love, wisdom, and essence carry forward, even if their form changes?

e. Integrating the Journey: Moving Into the Afterlife with Dignity and Hope

Contemplating a Gentle Crossing

- How can I envision a peaceful transition, supported by the loving presence of ancestors, angels, or spiritual beings welcoming me into a new realm?
- How does imagining my consciousness moving through luminous states, encountering divine light or cosmic oneness, help me release fear?

Leaving a Legacy of Faith and Understanding

- How might sharing my thoughts on the afterlife with loved ones reduce their anxiety and provide them with a framework of hope and continuity?
- How might my reflections on postmortem existence inspire others to consider their own beliefs, promoting open dialogue and spiritual exploration?

Trusting the Soul's Path

- How can I trust that the essence of my being, shaped by love and experience, will continue to evolve as I approach this profound threshold?
- What final affirmation or prayer might I offer, symbolizing my willingness to embrace whatever lies beyond death with courage, humility, and hope?

By contemplating these questions, you can engage deeply with the mysteries of what follows physical life. This introspection may foster acceptance, spiritual clarity, and an openness to possibilities beyond your limited understanding. Ultimately, facing mortality through this lens of afterlife and continuity of consciousness can bring comfort, meaning, and a sense of peace as you prepare for the journey ahead.

1.7. Acceptance and Surrender: Coming to terms with mortality, recognizing the limits of human control, and embracing the mystery of death.

Below is a set of reflective and introspective questions centered on the theme of "Acceptance and Surrender." The questions encourage you facing mortality to acknowledge your past experiences, examine your relationships, reconcile unfinished matters, and embrace the profound mystery of death with compassion and wisdom. Each subcategory highlights the universal human experience of gradually releasing control, discovering peace, and finding meaning in the final stage of life.

a. **Personal Experiences and Memories: Acknowledging the Journey and Embracing Mortality**

Revisiting Life's Milestones

- Which personal experiences—both joyous and painful—have most profoundly shaped my understanding of life's impermanence?
- In what moments did I catch a glimpse of life's brevity, prompting me to reconsider my priorities and approach to living?
- How have my encounters with loss, grief, or mortality in the past influenced my perspective as I face my own death?

Recognizing the Limits of Human Control

- What times in my life illustrate when I tried to control outcomes, only to discover that life moved in unexpected directions?
- What wisdom can I glean from realizing that much of what has transpired was beyond my ability to shape or command?
- How have surrender and acceptance played roles in my personal growth, even before considering the end of my life?

Honoring the Fullness of My Life Story

- How can I find peace in acknowledging that my life, with all its imperfections and achievements, is complete in its own unique way?
- In what ways can I celebrate the legacy of my journey rather than regret what I have not done?
- How does embracing the totality of my life's tapestry—both triumphs and trials—help me find tranquility at this stage?

b. **Relationships and Interpersonal Connections: Releasing Grievances and Celebrating Bonds**

Evaluating Personal Connections

- Which relationships have brought me the most love, support, and understanding, and how can I cherish them now?
- What relationships in my life are affected by lingering resentment, misunderstanding, or pain, and how might I work toward finding peace in them?
- How might accepting my mortality influence my desire to offer forgiveness or understanding to others, regardless of past grievances?

Expressions of Gratitude and Closure

- How can I express gratitude to the individuals who have enriched my life and acknowledge the ways they've shaped my spirit?
- What simple words of acknowledgment, thanks, or love do I wish to share with others before it is too late?
- How can speaking honestly, humbly, and lovingly now help me release tension and encourage acceptance in myself and others?

Releasing Expectations and Judgments

- What expectations did I hold of others or myself that remain unmet, and can I let them go with compassion?
- How does removing blame and regret from my relationships free me to depart in peace, knowing I have done my best?
- How can I acknowledge that every individual, including myself, has limitations, and find understanding and compassion in that truth?

c. Unfulfilled Goals and Unresolved Conflicts: Letting Go of What Could Have Been

Confronting Unfinished Aspirations

- Which dreams and ambitions remain incomplete, and can I find solace in knowing I contributed what I could?
- How does acknowledging my finite capacity and time help me understand that not all aspirations must be fulfilled to live a meaningful life?
- How can I release the pressure to achieve and instead honor the effort, intention, and passion that fueled my dreams?

Accepting Personal Limitations

- In what ways can I make peace with the fact that I cannot fix every problem, heal every wound, or achieve every goal?
- How might humility, rather than disappointment, guide me to accept my human boundaries as natural and even sacred?
- How can I reinterpret "unfinished business" as part of a larger, ongoing narrative that extends beyond my physical presence?

Transforming Regret into Understanding

- What regrets do I hold about words unspoken, opportunities missed, or conflicts left unresolved, and how can I soften these feelings with empathy for myself?
- How can I view my regrets as lessons that deepened my compassion, helping me face mortality with greater tenderness toward myself and others?

- How does recognizing the universal nature of imperfect lives help me accept my own story without condemnation?

d. The Search for Meaning and Reconciliation: Finding Spiritual Equilibrium

Seeking Meaning in Vulnerability

- As I surrender to life's impermanence, what profound meaning might I discover in my vulnerability and dependence on others?
- How can admitting that I do not have all the answers help me find spiritual strength and trust that truth may emerge through surrender?
- How might acknowledging that life is a gift, not a guarantee, inspire reverence, awe, and humility as I approach the unknown?

Connecting to Something Greater

- How do I sense a larger pattern, divine presence, or spiritual reality that transcends my individual existence as I contemplate death?
- What beliefs—personal or traditional—bring me comfort by suggesting a continuity of the spirit or a reunion with the divine or loved ones?
- How does trusting in a mystery beyond my control release the weight of trying to define, explain, or control what comes next?

Reconciliation with the Mystery of Death

- How can I approach death as a natural, sacred threshold that all living beings must cross, rather than resisting or fearing it?
- What practices or perspectives might help me cultivate a quiet acceptance, allowing feelings of anxiety or sadness to arise and dissipate, creating space for peace?
- How does admitting my lack of control and knowledge over what lies beyond help me embrace death as a meaningful passage rather than an unjust finality?

e. Integrating Acceptance and Surrender into the Final Moments

Embodying Peace in Each Breath

- How can I practice releasing tension and fear in the present moment, using my breath or prayer to invite calm acceptance?
- What helps me hold compassion for my body, mind, and spirit as I face my final days or hours, understanding that surrender can be a grace-filled release rather than a defeat?
- How does intentionally welcoming each moment—however challenging—prepare me for the ultimate surrender of life itself?

Leaving a Legacy of Acceptance

- How might my journey toward acceptance and surrender serve as a model or comfort for those I leave behind?
- How can I communicate to my loved ones that releasing control and embracing uncertainty is a profoundly human and noble act?
- What spiritual gift might I offer to others by meeting death with dignity, understanding, and peace, showing them how to one day walk this path?

Finding Serenity in Letting Go

- How does relinquishing the struggle to control outcomes help me discover a gentle freedom and spaciousness in my heart?
- What allows me to be fully present, letting every emotion, memory, and sensation pass through me without resistance?
- How can surrendering to mortality help me unite with a greater cosmic rhythm and open myself to whatever lies beyond with humility and grace?

By reflecting on these questions, you can nurture a sense of acceptance and surrender, transcending fear and resistance. This exploration encourages you to embrace the natural limits of human existence, find reconciliation in your relationships, and discover peace in the face of life's greatest mystery: the moment when control yields to trust, and life yields to whatever lies ahead.

Chapter 2. Emotional and Psychological Concerns

2.1. **Fear, Anxiety, and Uncertainty**: Acknowledging the natural fear of non-existence, pain, or leaving loved ones behind.

Below is a set of reflective questions centered on the theme of "Fear, Anxiety, and Uncertainty" as you approach the end of life. Organized into four main subcategories—Personal Experiences and Memories, Relationships and Interpersonal Connections, Unfulfilled Goals or Unresolved Conflicts, and The Search for Meaning and Reconciliation—these questions are designed to prompt deep introspection, acknowledge natural fears, and foster spiritual growth. They address the universal human experience of facing mortality, grappling with the unknown, and seeking understanding and peace.

a. Personal Experiences and Memories: Understanding the Roots of Fear

Acknowledging the Reality of Mortality

- When did I first become aware of my own mortality, and how have my feelings about it changed over time?
- Which personal experiences—illness, loss, accidents—most starkly reminded me that life is finite, and how have they shaped my current fears or anxieties?
- How have previous encounters with death—whether of family, friends, or public figures—influenced the way I now view the end of my own life?

Confronting the Unknown

- What aspects of death's mystery (non-existence, posthumous legacy, spiritual realms) trigger fear or uncertainty in me?
- What aspects of the dying process—such as the possibility of pain, loss of control, or the fading of consciousness—unsettle me most, and how do they compare to my feelings about death itself?
- What moments of courage, inner strength, or resilience from my past can reassure me that I can face these final transitions with grace?

Accepting Human Vulnerability

- How have I learned to accept vulnerability as a natural part of life, and how can I apply this acceptance to the ultimate vulnerability of death?
- What helps me find compassion for myself in acknowledging that feeling anxious or afraid is not a weakness, but a deeply human response to the unknown?
- How do my fears reflect my humanity—my attachment to life, my love for others, my longing for continuation?

b. **Relationships and Interpersonal Connections: Fears About Leaving Loved Ones Behind**

Separation and Loss

- Am I afraid of the pain my loved ones will feel when I am gone, and how can I acknowledge their grief while still finding peace in my own passing?
- What worries me most about leaving family and friends behind—will they be cared for, will they remember me lovingly, will they move forward with strength and support?
- How can I accept that, while I cannot control how others cope with my loss, my expressions of love and guidance now may ease their future sorrow?

Honest Communication and Reassurance

- What difficult conversations have I avoided that might help lessen the fear of future misunderstandings or regrets for those I leave behind?
- How can I entrust certain loved ones or spiritual mentors to carry forth my memory and values, reassuring myself that a part of me will live on in their hearts?
- How might sharing my fears openly help strengthen the bond with my loved ones and remind me that I am not alone in this experience?

Cultivating a Peaceful Legacy

- How can I clarify my spiritual, emotional, or practical wishes to calm both my mind and the minds of those who may feel confusion or uncertainty in my absence?
- How does viewing my relationships as eternal—through love, memory, or spiritual connection—help reduce my fear of absolute separation?
- How might leaving a letter, a message, or a blessing help ease my anxiety by ensuring my loved ones know they were cherished and that I found peace in my final days?

c. **Unfulfilled Goals or Unresolved Conflicts: Addressing Fears of Incompletion**

Acknowledging What Remains Undone

- Which unfulfilled ambitions or postponed dreams weigh heaviest on my heart, intensifying my fear that I have not fully realized my potential?
- How can I accept that life rarely allows us to complete every goal and that my worth is not solely defined by checked boxes or final achievements?
- How might I reinterpret "incompletion" as part of a larger human story, one in which everyone leaves something undone?

Releasing Regrets and Tensions

- What lingering conflicts or unresolved tensions with others might be exacerbating my anxiety about leaving this world without setting things right?
- How can I use letters, phone calls, prayers, or silent forgiveness to address these unresolved matters and lighten my emotional burden?
- What would it mean to grant myself mercy and understanding for not having resolved every conflict, trusting that my intentions and efforts matter more than perfect closure?

Transforming Goals into Lessons Learned

- How might acknowledging my unfulfilled goals help me appreciate the growth, learning, or relationships formed in their pursuit, rather than focusing on their incompletion?

- What comfort can I find in knowing that the wisdom I've gained will remain meaningful, even if I cannot see every vision realized?
- How does viewing life's trajectory as ongoing beyond physical death—through spiritual evolution or the influence I've had on others—ease my fears about leaving projects or aspirations incomplete?

d. The Search for Meaning and Reconciliation: Finding Inner Peace Amid Uncertainty

Reflecting on Core Values and Beliefs

- How might reconnecting with my deepest values—love, kindness, service, faith—reassure me that my life held purpose and value, easing the fear of oblivion?
- What spiritual framework, religious teaching, or philosophical perspective brings me comfort by suggesting that death is not the end but a transition or transformation?
- How might contemplating divine compassion, universal love, or the continuity of consciousness soften my fear of non-existence and inspire hope in something greater?

Embracing Mystery and Letting Go of Control

- How can accepting that not all questions have clear answers help me embrace life's mystery and bring quiet peace to my anxious mind?
- How might surrendering to the truth of uncertainty become an act of faith, trust, and courage, rather than a feeling of defeat?
- How does releasing the need to control outcomes—my health, the circumstances of my death, the future of my loved ones—free me to live my remaining time more fully, savoring each moment?

Cultivating Spiritual Resilience and Gratitude

- What spiritual practices—such as prayer, meditation, or reflective reading—help me acknowledge fear while allowing gratitude for the life I have lived to take precedence?
- How can I reconcile with my mortality by affirming that my existence, however brief, has contributed to the tapestry of humanity and that this legacy endures despite the darkness of uncertainty?
- How does focusing on the love I have shared, the kindness I have shown, and the understanding I have developed give me a sense of meaning that transcends fear?

By engaging with these questions, you can navigate the profound and natural fears that arise as your life's end draws near. This introspective journey may help transform anxiety into acceptance, fear into understanding, and uncertainty into a poignant reminder of what it means to be fully human, guided by love, meaning, and the quiet dignity of embracing life's final mystery.

2.2. **Grief and Sadness**: Allowing space for sorrow over unrealized dreams, future milestones missed, and the end of physical life.

Below is a set of introspective questions focused on the theme of **Grief and Sadness** as one approaches the end of life. The questions are organized into meaningful subcategories that prompt you to acknowledge and give space to sorrow—whether it stems from personal memories, unfulfilled ambitions, or relationships. Each question encourages honest self-examination, emotional growth, and spiritual healing, ultimately helping individuals reconcile with their experiences and find peace.

a. **Personal Experiences and Memories: Honoring the Fullness of a Life Lived**

Acknowledging Loss and Letting Go

- What aspects of my life do I grieve leaving behind—cherished routines, familiar spaces, or long-held passions?
- Which memories bring both joy and sadness, reminding me that I am saying farewell to experiences that cannot be replicated?
- How can I honor these memories, perhaps by reflecting on them quietly, sharing stories with loved ones, or engaging in a final ritual that commemorates my journey?

Embracing Emotional Authenticity

- How can I allow myself to fully feel my sorrow without rushing to suppress or justify it?
- What helps me accept tears and longing as valid expressions of love, appreciation, and the human condition, rather than viewing them as signs of weakness?
- How do I balance acknowledging my sadness over what I must leave with gratitude for what I've been fortunate enough to have known and loved?

Finding Strength in Vulnerability

- How can recognizing sadness as a natural response to approaching life's end help me see it as evidence of the depth and significance of my life?
- How does acknowledging my sorrow open my heart to greater compassion for myself and others who face loss and change
- How might recognizing the fragility of existence help me appreciate the preciousness of each moment that remains?

b. **Relationships and Interpersonal Connections: Grieving the Future and Treasuring the Past**

Mourning Future Absences

- Which future milestones—celebrations, graduations, weddings, or births—do I sorrowfully acknowledge I will not witness?
- How can I convey my love, encouragement, and hopes to those I will leave behind, so they carry something of me into their futures?
- How can creating a legacy of understanding or support ease my sadness, knowing that my influence will persist even in my physical absence?

Reflecting on Shared History

- Which relationships have sustained me, and how does it feel to know I'm stepping away from these treasured bonds?
- How can I balance grieving the inevitable parting with feeling gratitude for the meaningful connections that have enriched my life?
- What words of appreciation, apologies, or blessings can I share with loved ones to bring a sense of completion and ease the weight of unspoken sorrow?

Accepting the Imperfections of Relationships

- Do unresolved conflicts or misunderstandings deepen my sadness, and how can I seek understanding or forgiveness to alleviate this pain?
- How can I accept that not all relationships will be perfectly mended, and view the presence of sadness as a reflection of the complexity and importance of these connections?
- How might offering compassion to myself and others help heal lingering emotional wounds and soften grief as I approach my farewell?

c. **Unfulfilled Goals and Unresolved Conflicts: Mourning What Could Have Been**

Confronting Unfinished Dreams

- Which aspirations and goals remain unrealized, and what sadness arises from the knowledge that I must let them go?
- How can I acknowledge the finiteness of human life and accept that few achieve all they hope for, without diminishing the worth of my efforts and intentions?
- What comfort can I find in knowing that even my unfulfilled dreams have shaped my character, taught me resilience, and guided my growth?

Finding Meaning in Incompletion

- How could I reinterpret sadness over unfinished work as a sign of how deeply I cared and how boldly I dared to dream and strive?
- How can I accept that life's beauty often lies in its imperfections, and view sorrow over what could have been as part of the profound truth of being human?
- How might I trust that others, inspired by me or influenced by my values, may carry forward some of my hopes, thus softening my grief?

Releasing the Burden of Regret

- What regrets sharpen my sadness—things I wish I'd said or done differently—and how can I find a way to forgive myself?
- How can I speak words of understanding, even in my own heart, to release regrets and focus on the love, effort, and sincerity I brought to life's challenges?
- How does acknowledging that everyone carries some regrets help me feel less isolated in my sadness, making space for self-compassion?

d. The Search for Meaning and Reconciliation: Transcending Grief Through Understanding

Contemplating Life's Transience

- How does confronting sadness over my impending absence encourage me to look beyond the material world toward spiritual or philosophical truths?
- How might reflecting on the impermanence of all things—seasons changing, generations passing—give context to my sorrow and connect me to the universal human experience?
- In what ways can I find solace in a spiritual understanding, faith tradition, or sense of cosmic order that frames my sadness as part of a larger divine or natural design?

Cultivating Inner Peace Amid Sorrow

- How can I hold both sadness and peace simultaneously, understanding that one does not exclude the other?
- How does recognizing that sadness can coexist with love, wisdom, and hope guide me toward inner harmony rather than despair?
- How might prayer, meditation, music, art, or sacred readings help me transform sorrow into a source of quiet strength and acceptance?

Reconciling with the End of Physical Life

- What helps me acknowledge my sadness over leaving this physical existence while trusting in the possibility of something beyond—such as spiritual continuity, remembered legacy, or the ripple effects of my life's actions?
- How might embracing sorrow gently, without resistance, enable me to approach death with greater honesty, courage, and openness?
- How might the integration of grief into my farewell bring a sense of completion, ensuring I step toward the unknown with authenticity, humility, and a heart that has fully loved and fully mourned?

By contemplating these questions, you may find that grief and sadness are not merely weights to carry but pathways to greater self-awareness, compassion, and spiritual growth. In allowing space for sorrow—over unrealized dreams, missed future milestones, and the end of physical life—they affirm the depth of your humanity and the significance of your journey. Ultimately, embracing this sadness can lead to profound understanding, gentle reconciliation, and a more peaceful acceptance of life's natural conclusion.

2.3. **Guilt, Regret, and Forgiveness**: Facing past mistakes, seeking forgiveness (from oneself, others, and the divine), and offering forgiveness to those who have caused harm.

Below is a set of reflective, introspective questions focused on the theme of Guilt, Regret, and Forgiveness as you approach the end of life. Each subcategory is designed to encourage honest self-examination, foster inner reconciliation, and inspire spiritual growth. These questions guide individuals through examining personal memories, relationships, unfulfilled aspirations, and the broader spiritual search for meaning, ultimately helping to release burdens, seek forgiveness, and embrace compassion.

a. **Personal Experiences and Memories: Unearthing Roots of Guilt and Regret**

Recognizing Past Mistakes and Shortcomings

- Which past decisions, words, or actions do I feel most guilty or regretful about, and what specific outcomes or harms arose from them?
- How did fear, insecurity, pride, or misunderstanding influence my choices at the time, and can I empathize now with the person I was then?
- Have I allowed myself to fully acknowledge the pain or disappointment I caused—both to myself and others—and can I face this truth with honesty and courage?

Understanding the Context of Actions

- What circumstances—emotional, cultural, or situational—led me toward actions or omissions that now weigh on my conscience?

- How might recognizing my own limitations and vulnerabilities at that time help me view my mistakes with greater compassion and understanding?
- How can I revisit these memories and separate my worth as a human being from the imperfections of my past behavior?

Transforming Regret into Insight

- What lessons can I extract from my regrets, and how have they shaped my moral compass, guiding me toward growth and greater wisdom?
- How might acknowledging my imperfections strengthen my humility, empathy, and dedication to doing good, even now?
- How can I view these difficult memories as opportunities for personal evolution, rather than as permanent stains on my character?

b. ## Relationships and Interpersonal Connections: Seeking and Offering Forgiveness

Asking Forgiveness from Others

- Who are the individuals I have harmed, disappointed, or misled, and how might I approach offering an apology or explanation to them?
- How can I muster the courage to reach out to these individuals, if possible, or hold them in my heart with sincere remorse, hoping they find healing?
- What would it feel like to lay down my defenses, pride, or fear of judgment and simply acknowledge my wrongdoing and regret?

Granting Forgiveness to Those Who Caused Harm

- Who are the people whose actions or words left me wounded, and how might withholding forgiveness have allowed me to hold onto anger or a sense of moral superiority?
- How can I understand that forgiving does not excuse the harm done but instead frees me from the heavy burden of resentment and bitterness?
- How can I release those who hurt me in my heart, even if I cannot directly communicate forgiveness, trusting that this inner act of grace will benefit my own spirit?

Finding Balance in Complex Relationships

- How might owning my mistakes without blaming myself entirely and forgiving others without dismissing my pain help restore balance to my emotional landscape?
- How do I recognize that every human relationship carries a mixture of love, misunderstanding, kindness, and hurt, and how can forgiveness honor this complexity?

- How can approaching forgiveness as a two-way process—seeking it where I've done harm and offering it where I've been harmed—bring greater harmony to my final days?

c. **Unfulfilled Goals, Unresolved Conflicts, and Incomplete Stories**

Letting Go of Unfinished Conversations

- What unresolved conflicts, unspoken words, or unmended fences remain in my life, and how can I find closure within myself now?
- How might imagining what I would say if given the chance, and articulating these thoughts through prayer, letters, or spoken intentions, help me release lingering guilt or anger?
- How might acknowledging that not all stories can have a perfect resolution allow me to accept imperfection and move forward with a lighter spirit?

Accepting Limitations and Imperfections

- What remorse do I carry for not living up to my own standards or failing to meet the moral or personal ideals I once set for myself?
- How can I forgive myself for being human—for not always knowing what I know now and for not always having the emotional resources to act differently?
- How does understanding the inevitability of unfulfilled dreams and incomplete healing help me approach death with more compassion and less self-condemnation?

Finding Peace in the Face of Incompletion

- How can I trust that my sincere wish to make amends or do better, even if partially unrealized, still holds meaning?
- How might releasing the need for absolute resolution free me from guilt, allowing me to find spiritual peace and accept the flow of life as it is?
- How might acknowledging that everyone leaves unfinished chapters behind help me feel less alone in my regrets and more connected to the shared human experience?

d. **The Search for Meaning and Reconciliation: Embracing Divine Mercy and Spiritual Growth**

Seeking Forgiveness from the Divine

- If I hold a belief in the divine, how might I approach that sacred presence now—through prayer, reflection, confession—asking for understanding and mercy?

- How do I connect with a loving force, higher power, or universal grace that can absorb and transform my regrets, offering unconditional forgiveness?
- How can I entrust my wounds, mistakes, and remorse to something greater than myself, finding solace in the idea that divine compassion exceeds human judgment?

Cultivating Self-Forgiveness and Compassion

- How can I grant myself the kindness I might freely offer a friend in my situation, recognizing that I deserve my own forgiveness as well?
- How can I view self-forgiveness not as an act of selfishness, but as a step toward wholeness and spiritual well-being?
- How might forgiving myself enable me to approach death not as someone condemned by past errors, but as a soul who has grown wiser through trials and repentance?

Reframing Guilt and Regret as Spiritual Teachers

- In what ways can guilt and regret serve as teachers, guiding me toward greater ethical clarity, empathy, and humility as I contemplate life's end?
- How does integrating forgiveness into my worldview—acknowledging that everyone, including myself, struggles and sometimes fails—enrich my spiritual maturity?
- How might embracing forgiveness deepen my trust in a moral or spiritual order, showing me that grace, healing, and redemption are possible even in the face of death?

By engaging deeply with these questions, you can confront your guilt and regrets, transforming them into catalysts for empathy, maturity, and spiritual healing. Seeking forgiveness from yourself, others, and the divine, as well as offering it to those who have caused harm, opens the path toward inner peace. Approaching death with a reconciled heart fosters a sense of liberation, dignity, and wholeness, ensuring that your final chapters are not defined by remorse but illuminated by understanding, compassion, and grace.

2.4. **Sense of Peace and Inner Calm**: Striving to find emotional balance, tranquility, and healing in one's final chapter.

Below is a set of reflective and introspective questions focused on the theme of "Sense of Peace and Inner Calm." These questions guide you through personal experiences, relationships, unfulfilled aspirations, and the quest for meaning, ultimately encouraging emotional balance, healing, and spiritual growth as you approach life's end. Each category is designed to help you acknowledge the past, accept the present, and open your heart to the possibility of peace.

a. **Personal Experiences and Memories: Embracing the Full Tapestry of Life**

Honoring Life's Journey

- Which moments in my life brought me profound peace or a feeling of being in harmony with myself and the world?
- What times have I overcome hardship and found unexpected inner strength, and how do these memories reassure me in this moment?
- What simple pleasures—such as walks in nature, quiet evenings at home, or shared laughter—can I recall that calm my spirit when remembered?

Accepting Imperfections

- How can I embrace the idea that my life, with all its successes and struggles, forms a complete tapestry that is inherently worthy and valuable?
- How does recognizing that no life is without pain or mistakes help me release unrealistic expectations, making room for serenity?
- What lessons can I find within my regrets and heartaches, and how might they deepen my compassion toward myself and others?

Finding Peace in Reflection

- How does taking a few moments each day to reflect on what I have learned and appreciated bring me closer to a state of calm acceptance?
- In what ways can I practice gratitude for the experiences I've had, even those that were challenging, as part of my soul's growth?
- How might gentle introspection—through prayer, journaling, meditation—restore my sense of inner equilibrium?

b. **Relationships and Interpersonal Connections: Cultivating Harmony with Others**

Cherishing Supportive Bonds

- Which relationships have consistently nurtured and uplifted me, and how can recalling their love settle my heart?
- How can I express gratitude to those who have cared for me, thereby strengthening bonds of mutual understanding and peace?
- How can the knowledge that I've positively touched others' lives reassure me that my presence has truly mattered?

Fostering Understanding and Forgiveness

- What lingering tensions or misunderstandings can I seek to resolve, or come to terms with internally, to lighten my emotional load?
- How can releasing resentment or regret by viewing others with greater empathy, and understanding that everyone carries their own burdens, bring me peace?
- How does offering or seeking forgiveness clear a path to inner tranquility, soothing the unrest that may block my peace?

Embracing Love and Connection

- How can recognizing that love and goodwill endure beyond physical presence help me trust that bonds will outlast the confines of mortality?
- How might envisioning loved ones continuing their lives with the strength and lessons I've imparted calm my worries about leaving them behind?
- What helps me hold onto a sense of community—family, friends, and mentors—that assures me I am not alone, even as I approach the end?

c. Unfulfilled Goals and Unresolved Conflicts: Making Peace with Imperfection

Acknowledging Incompletion

- Which dreams remain unfulfilled, and can I accept that not all aspirations need to be realized for my life to be meaningful?
- How can I find solace in recognizing that even unrealized goals have guided my character, values, and growth?
- How can I cherish the effort and intention I invested, rather than fixating on what remains undone?

Confronting Lingering Discomfort

- What unresolved inner conflicts—fears, insecurities, or regrets—do I carry, and how can I approach them with compassion?
- In what ways can acknowledging these unresolved issues—rather than denying them—bring healing and calm to my inner landscape?
- How might reflective practices, such as prayer, conversations with a trusted confidant, or spiritual counsel, help me address these conflicts, even symbolically, to restore equilibrium?

Releasing the Burden of Regret

- How can I forgive myself for not meeting every standard I once set, recognizing that I did my best with the understanding I had at the time?

- In what ways can I frame my regrets as stepping stones to deeper insight and humility, rather than viewing them as failures?
- How does letting go of self-judgment and embracing self-acceptance create more space for peaceful surrender?

d. The Search for Meaning and Reconciliation: Finding Spiritual Anchors

Exploring Spiritual Anchors

- What spiritual or philosophical beliefs resonate with my heart, and how can connecting with these beliefs steady me in uncertain times?
- How can viewing life and death as natural chapters in a broader cosmic or divine design bring me comfort and ease my fears and insecurities?
- How might prayer, sacred readings, chanting, or time in nature help anchor me in a sense of the sacred, quieting inner turmoil?

Aligning with Core Values

- What values—kindness, honesty, service, love—have guided me through life, and can reaffirming them now foster inner tranquility?
- How do I see my life as part of a greater moral or spiritual tapestry, where my contributions, however modest, hold significance?
- How can reflecting on the love, understanding, and wisdom I've fostered remind me that my life has had meaningful purpose?

Embracing Mystery with Grace

- How can I accept that not all questions have clear answers and find peace in surrendering to mystery?
- How does acknowledging life's inherent uncertainty free me from the need to control outcomes and instead rest in trust and patience?
- What helps me greet the unknown with a quiet heart, finding comfort in the idea that peace resides not in certainty, but in acceptance?

e. Integrating Peace into the Final Chapter: Living and Leaving with Serenity

Cultivating Daily Calm

- What small daily practices—mindful breathing, a short prayer, listening to soothing music—help me maintain inner balance as I approach the end?
- How can focusing on the present moment—rather than fretting over the past or future—ground me in a serene awareness of life as it is now?
- How can embracing simplicity by letting go of unnecessary worries, tasks, or conflicts create space for genuine calm?

Leaving a Legacy of Serenity

- Does knowing that my demeanor and acceptance may inspire others encourage me to foster serenity within myself, as a final gift to them?
- How can clarifying my wishes, sharing my reflections, and offering blessings to loved ones bring a sense of purposeful closure?
- How c an you envision a peaceful transition—surrounded by gratitude, understanding, and love—help ease anxiety and tension?

Welcoming the Final Surrender

- How does knowing that my demeanor and acceptance may inspire others encourage me to cultivate serenity within myself as a final gift to them?
- How does embracing the inevitability of departure free me from resistance, allowing grace and tranquility to fill my heart?
- How can I step forward with gentle assurance, recognizing that I have done what I could, loved as I could, and grown as I could, making space now for rest and peace?

By engaging with these questions, you may gradually find greater emotional balance, tranquility, and healing in your final chapters of life. Each question encourages a deeper understanding of yourself, your relationships, and your place in the broader spiritual and cosmic tapestry. Embracing these inquiries can lead to profound inner calm, allowing you to approach life's conclusion with courage, grace, and a wellspring of peace.

2.5. **Hope and Comfort**: Finding inner resources that alleviate emotional turmoil—whether through prayer, nature, art, music, or meditation.

Below is a set of reflective and introspective questions focused on the theme of "Hope and Comfort." These questions are designed to guide you toward uncovering inner resources that can alleviate emotional turmoil in your final stage of life. Organized into meaningful subcategories, they encourage deep reflection on personal history, relationships, unfulfilled goals, and spiritual understanding. Each question aims to foster spiritual growth, emotional resilience, and the discovery of sources of solace—whether found in prayer, nature, art, music, meditation, or other personal practices.

a. **Personal Experiences and Memories: Tapping Into Past Sources of Hope**

Recalling Comforting Moments

- What times in my life did I feel most supported, understood, or at peace, and can I draw on those memories now?
- Which personal achievements, no matter how small, have brought me a sense of inner pride and reassurance when I've felt uncertain?

- What moments in nature—such as sunsets, quiet forests, or gentle rivers—can I revisit in my mind to inspire calm and faith in life's cycles?

Identifying Sustaining Practices

- Which practices—journaling, painting, listening to music, daily prayer—have reliably comforted me in the past?
- How did creative outlets or hobbies once help me navigate hardships, and can rekindling these interests now provide hope?
- What spiritual or religious rituals—such as lighting a candle, repeating a mantra, or reading a sacred text—have anchored me during difficult times, and how might they support me now?

Acknowledging Resilience

- When have I overcome despair or anxiety before, and what inner strengths did I discover within myself?
- How might recognizing my own resilience assure me that I can approach this final chapter with courage and grace?
- How can I frame challenging past experiences as lessons that enriched my character and expanded my capacity for hope?

b. **Relationships and Interpersonal Connections: Drawing Strength from Bonds**

Support from Loved Ones

- Who are the people, past or present, who have brought comfort and encouragement into my life, and how does their memory or presence steady me now?
- How can recalling the ways I've been cared for and loved reassure me that I am cherished and connected, even as I near life's end?
- How might imagining loved ones continuing my legacy of kindness, wisdom, or creativity soothe my fears and inspire hope?

Sharing Comfort and Gratitude

- How can expressing appreciation to those who have supported me lighten my heart and create moments of shared solace?
- What gestures—such as writing letters, recording messages, or offering prayers—can I make for loved ones to affirm the enduring power of our bond and provide mutual comfort?
- How can acknowledging the love and empathy exchanged between us assure me that I am never truly alone?

Rekindling Forgiveness and Understanding

- How can extending understanding or forgiveness for unresolved tensions reduce emotional burdens and create space for hope?
- How does recognizing that all human relationships are marked by imperfection help me find compassion and comfort in our shared frailty?
- What steps can I take to release anger or resentment in favor of empathy, allowing comforting emotions—like acceptance and tenderness—to flourish?

c. Unfulfilled Goals and Unresolved Conflicts: Finding Hope in Acceptance

Embracing Incompleteness

- How can I find comfort in knowing that few lives unfold perfectly and that unachieved goals do not diminish my worth or legacy?
- How might reframing my unfulfilled aspirations as seeds planted for others' future growth bring me a quiet sense of purpose?
- What freedom might I gain by accepting that not every conflict can be neatly resolved, allowing me to focus on what truly matters now?

Seeking Growth Through Release

- What dreams can I symbolically release with compassion, recognizing that my sincere efforts held meaning regardless of their outcome?
- How might acknowledging my inability to control all aspects of life's trajectory remind me that grace often lies in surrender rather than achievement?
- What space might letting go of certain expectations create within me for renewed hope, peace, and spiritual insight?

Transforming Regret into Understanding

- How can I transform regret into understanding, viewing it as part of the human condition, to find gentle acceptance and calm?
- How might allowing myself to mourn unmet desires help me process sadness and create a more honest, compassionate narrative of my life?
- What deeper sense of hope might I discover by admitting life's inherent imperfections and embracing authenticity and truth?

d. The Search for Meaning and Reconciliation: Discovering Spiritual Anchors

Connecting with the Sacred or Divine

- How can I reaffirm my connection to the divine through practices such as prayer, meditation, or reading sacred texts that console and uplift me?
- How might feeling part of something larger—a universal love, a cosmic order, or a spiritual community—quell fears and foster hope?
- What helps me imagine my existence as part of a greater tapestry, where the threads of my life continue to influence and harmonize with others?

Drawing on Symbolic and Artistic Expressions

- What paintings, songs, poems, or sacred symbols evoke serenity and inspire confidence that life's beauty endures beyond physical form?
- How does art, music, or poetry help me name emotions that feel too vast for ordinary words, offering solace through expression rather than explanation?
- How might meditating on inspiring imagery—such as sunrises, mandalas, or icons—help me ground myself in a calm and hopeful mindset that transcends fear?

Embracing the Mystery with Trust

- How can I accept that some questions will remain unanswered and find comfort in embracing mystery rather than seeking certainty?
- How does trusting that life's intangible qualities—love, learning, virtue—hold value beyond my earthly presence bring reassurance?
- What helps me envision my passing not as an end, but as a transition, nourished by faith, imagination, and the belief in enduring goodness?

e. ## Integrating Hope and Comfort into Final Moments: Nurturing Inner Peace

Establishing Daily Practices of Comfort

- What simple daily rituals—lighting a candle, reciting a calming phrase, sitting quietly in nature—can infuse hope and comfort into my remaining time?
- How can adopting a mindful approach to each moment—savoring breaths, sensations, and kind words—help me build a refuge of calm within myself?
- How might focusing on the present—rather than anxieties of the future or regrets of the past—nurture a healing sense of ease?

Sharing Wisdom and Blessings

- How might offering blessings or parting words of encouragement and insight to loved ones solidify a sense of hopeful legacy, bringing comfort to both them and me?
- How does imparting what I've learned—my values, stories, and inspirations—reaffirm the positive impact I leave behind, fueling hope that my essence lives on in others' hearts?
- How can I welcome resources such as prayer, nature, art, music, or meditation to bring comfort, trusting that hope can arise from many wells?What assurance can I find in knowing that having earnestly searched for meaning and solace makes approaching life's threshold less daunting?

By contemplating these questions, you can discover and strengthen your inner sources of hope and comfort. These reflections encourage turning toward what has historically eased pain, fostered understanding, and brought peace—be it faith, creativity, nature, relationships, or spiritual rituals. Engaging with these inquiries can help transform uncertainty and emotional turmoil into a more peaceful, hopeful stance, guiding the soul gently toward life's final embrace.

Chapter 3. Social and Relational Dimensions

3.1. Reconciliation and Closure: Mending strained relationships, expressing love, gratitude, and unfinished sentiments.

Below is a set of reflective, introspective questions centered on the theme of Reconciliation and Closure. These questions encourage you to honestly examine you personal histories, relationships, unfulfilled goals, and the deeper search for meaning as they approach life's end. Each subcategory is designed to foster emotional healing, spiritual growth, and the emergence of genuine understanding and love. By engaging with these questions, you may find a path toward mending strained connections, expressing gratitude, and finding peace in your final chapters.

a. **Personal Experiences and Memories: Acknowledging the Roots of Unfinished Business**

Reflecting on Past Events

- Which life events or decisions still weigh heavily on my heart, leaving me with a sense of unfinished resolution?

- What personal disappointments or regrets—choices I made or didn't make—linger within me, and how might I address or find peace with them?
- How can acknowledging my own vulnerabilities, fears, or misunderstandings at the time help me view these events with greater compassion?

Embracing the Complexity of My Story

- What recurring patterns—such as avoidance, anger, or pride—do I notice in my past, and how might they have hindered reconciliation?
- How has my cultural, spiritual, or family background influenced the way I approached conflicts or expressed emotions?
- How does recognizing that I've done the best I could with the tools and understanding I had at the time help soften my self-judgment?

b. Relationships and Interpersonal Connections: Healing Rifts and Deepening Bonds

Revisiting Important Relationships

- Whose face comes to mind when I think of unresolved tension, hurtful words, or painful silences?
- What relationships that were once close have grown distant due to misunderstandings, unspoken resentments, or changing circumstances, and how might I approach them with understanding or closure?
- Which individuals—even those no longer present in my life—might benefit from my acknowledgment, apology, or well-wishing?

Expressing Love, Gratitude, and Appreciation

- To whom do I owe words of gratitude or love that I haven't yet spoken? How might sharing these sentiments ease my heart and theirs?
- What specific qualities, acts of kindness, or lessons imparted by others have influenced who I've become, and how can I honor their impact on my life?
- In what ways can I express appreciation sincerely and specifically, so that the other person knows their presence deeply mattered?

Bridging Distance Through Honest Communication

- What conversations have I avoided out of fear, pride, or uncertainty, and what might be gained by initiating those talks now?
- How can I listen to others' perspectives more openly, acknowledging that both my truth and their truth may hold validity?

- What steps can I take—such as writing letters, recording messages, or praying on their behalf—to seek reconciliation when face-to-face communication isn't possible, and how might this entrust my sentiments to time, spirit, or memory?

c. Unfulfilled Goals and Unresolved Conflicts: Seeking Inner Resolution

Acknowledging Unfinished Aspirations

- What shared dreams or plans with others—such as family trips, projects, or long-deferred conversations—will go unrealized, and how can I reflect on their significance?
- How might accepting these unfulfilled goals help me recognize that some forms of reconciliation involve embracing imperfection and letting go?
- How can I find meaning in the intentions and love behind these uncompleted endeavors, viewing them as expressions of care rather than failures?

Making Peace with Regrets

- What regrets persist—such as words left unsaid, apologies withheld, or opportunities missed—and how can I begin to articulate them now, even if only in my heart?
- How can recognizing that forgiveness involves releasing myself from guilt and freeing others from blame help me find greater peace?
- How can transforming regret into understanding or compassion help me see my past shortcomings as steps along a human journey rather than final verdicts?

Confronting Inner Resistance

- What inner barriers—fear of rejection, reluctance to appear weak, lingering anger—prevent me from seeking reconciliation?
- How can I gently challenge the barriers I hold by asking whether clinging to them truly serves my well-being or spiritual growth?
- How might reframing vulnerability as strength help me view reconciliation not as defeat, but as a courageous act of healing?

d. The Search for Meaning and Reconciliation: Integrating Love, Acceptance, and Spiritual Insight

Aligning with Core Values

- Which spiritual or moral principles guide me—love, compassion, humility, forgiveness—and how can I bring them to bear on mending broken connections?

- How does affirming my values remind me that reconciliation is not just an emotional goal but also a spiritual calling that honors my deeper convictions?
- How might aligning my actions now with these values provide lasting solace and a more peaceful legacy?

Trusting in Divine or Cosmic Order

- How can believing in a divine presence, higher power, or cosmic balance help me surrender unresolved matters into loving hands greater than my own?
- What allows me to trust that even incomplete reconciliations have meaning in the grand tapestry of existence and that my sincere efforts carry weight?
- How does acknowledging life's mystery help me accept that some healing may unfold beyond my immediate perception, perhaps after I'm gone?

Embracing the Universality of Human Imperfection

- How does recognizing that everyone struggles with misunderstandings, regrets, and failures help me feel greater empathy for myself and others?
- What helps me view reconciliation as a universal human need—a shared endeavor to mend hearts that transcends individual circumstances?
- How might embracing this broader perspective instill a sense of peace, knowing I'm part of a collective journey toward understanding and love?

e. Moving Forward with Reconciliation and Closure: Leaving a Legacy of Compassion

Crafting a Personal Ritual of Closure

- What meaningful gestures—such as lighting a candle, saying a prayer, or meditating with photographs—might help me symbolically release old wounds?
- How might formal acts—like writing letters of apology, offering spoken blessings, or sharing meals—tangibly manifest reconciliation and bring comfort?
- How might these rituals serve as guideposts, ensuring I approach my final days with sincerity, integrity, and openheartedness?

Passing on Lessons Learned

- What wisdom about forgiveness, love, and healing can I impart to future generations, friends, or loved ones, so my experiences guide others?
- How can leaving behind a message of compassion—whether written or spoken—help me transform my personal struggles into collective insight?
- How does sharing my journey encourage others to seek reconciliation in their own lives, nurturing a ripple effect of understanding and goodwill?

By engaging with these questions, you may navigate the profound and tender work of reconciliation and closure. Through honest self-inquiry, you can acknowledge past wounds, express genuine love and gratitude, and find peace in embracing life's inherent complexities. These reflections offer a path toward mending relational threads, soothing old hurts, and departing with a balanced, open heart that reflects the best of your shared humanity.

3.2. **Family Communication and Bonds**: Ensuring open, honest conversations with family members, clarifying final wishes, and creating shared understanding.

Below is a set of reflective, introspective questions focused on Family Communication and Bonds as you approach the end of life. These questions are designed to guide you in examining your past experiences, current relationships, unfulfilled goals, and deeper spiritual yearnings related to your family. By carefully considering these questions, you can foster honest dialogues, clarify final wishes, and strengthen familial understanding, ultimately contributing to emotional healing and spiritual growth.

a. **Reflecting on the Past: Shared Histories and Legacies**

Honoring Family Memories

- Which moments shared with my family stand out as some of the most meaningful—celebrations, travels, quiet evenings, supportive gestures—and how can I acknowledge these memories openly?
- What family traditions, stories, or lessons passed down through generations do I want to reaffirm, and how can I ensure they live on after I am gone?
- How might recalling our collective past—both joyful and painful—help my loved ones understand where we have come from and where we might go together?

Recognizing Family Influences

- In what ways have my family members influenced my values, personality, and worldview, and can acknowledging their contributions encourage deeper respect and gratitude?

- What traits, talents, or passions have I inherited or nurtured within my family, and how can celebrating these continuities strengthen our bonds?
- Which elders or ancestors do I wish to honor, and how can I express how their memory and guidance continue to shape our family's path?

b. Understanding Current Family Dynamics: Forging Honest and Compassionate Connections

Open Communication and Vulnerability

- How honest and clear have I been in expressing my feelings, fears, and hopes to my family members, and what might have held me back—pride, fear, or misunderstanding?
- How can I encourage my family members to share their thoughts and emotions, assuring them that I value their perspectives and long for mutual understanding?
- How can I create a safe space for everyone to speak openly, listen deeply, and affirm one another's feelings without judgment?

Reevaluating Roles and Responsibilities

- How have I recognized and respected the changing roles within the family—such as children becoming caregivers or siblings taking on new responsibilities—as we navigate this transition?
- What imbalances or misunderstandings regarding caregiving duties, decision-making, or emotional support can I clarify or address to ease tensions?
- How can I affirm that each family member's contribution, no matter how small, is valuable and help us approach these final days with unity rather than strain?

c. Addressing Unfulfilled Goals, Unresolved Conflicts, and Lingering Regrets

Acknowledging Unspoken Tensions

- What unspoken hurts, resentments, or disappointments have I left unaddressed, and how might carefully initiating conversations now help lift emotional burdens?
- How can admitting my own mistakes, misunderstandings, or silences that contributed to family friction allow me to humbly seek forgiveness or understanding?
- How might extending empathy and compassion to others, even if conflicts remain partially unresolved, ease the family's sense of turmoil and pave the way for healing?

Accepting Imperfection and Incompletion

- How can I come to terms with the fact that not all familial conflicts may be neatly resolved, and how might partial understanding still bring peace?
- What family goals—such as reconciliations that never happened or dreams of togetherness that never fully materialized—can I release with acceptance and love?
- How does recognizing our shared humanity and vulnerability help me approach these unresolved matters with tenderness rather than regret?

d. Communicating Final Wishes and Practical Arrangements

Clarifying Wishes and Intentions

- How can I ensure that my healthcare preferences, funeral or memorial instructions, and other end-of-life decisions are clearly stated, so my family does not need to guess at my intentions?
- How can I present these plans not as demands but as offerings of clarity, love, and guidance meant to relieve their future uncertainty and stress?
- How might I encourage open dialogue about my final wishes, reassuring my family that their emotional comfort matters to me?

Ensuring Equitable Legacies

- What family heirlooms, keepsakes, letters, or spiritual blessings do I wish to distribute among loved ones, leaving them tangible or intangible gifts of my love and faith?
- How can I thoughtfully consider the emotional implications of my decisions and explain to each family member why I've chosen certain arrangements or distributions?
- How does ensuring transparency and fairness now cultivate trust, respect, and harmony within the family after I am gone?

e. The Search for Meaning, Reconciliation, and Spiritual Understanding

Conveying Values and Beliefs

- Which core values—love, compassion, generosity, resilience—do I hope my family will carry forward, and can I articulate these principles clearly?
- How might I share spiritual or religious insights, personal philosophies, or moral lessons that guided me, inspiring them to find their own spiritual grounding?
- How can I share how my faith or spiritual understanding provides comfort and context during this difficult time, while encouraging my family to find solace in their own ways?

Creating a Legacy of Understanding

- How might explaining the meaning I have found in both joyous and painful family chapters help my loved ones view our shared story with greater wisdom and acceptance?
- How can I invite my family to see my life's journey as part of a larger tapestry that continues through them, fostering a sense of continuity in the face of change?
- How does reassuring them that my love and presence transcend physical absence help ease their fears, offering hope that our bonds endure beyond mortal boundaries?

f.   Embracing the Future: Guiding the Family into the Next Chapter

Inviting Collaboration and Co-Creation

- How can I encourage my family members to work together and support each other after my death, emphasizing the importance of cherishing unity over division?
- How might discussing mutual goals, family traditions, or community service projects bring them closer, ensuring my departure does not leave a void but creates space for growth?
- What rituals—such as shared meals, annual gatherings, or moments of remembrance—can I suggest to honor my memory and strengthen their connections?

Letting Go with Grace and Love

- How can I express my trust in my loved ones' ability to navigate the future without me, imparting confidence and respect for their independent paths?
- How does demonstrating faith in their resilience and moral compass help me depart peacefully, knowing they will find strength in themselves and each other?
- What helps me embrace the mystery of life's transitions, surrender my worries, and leave my loved ones with blessings, gratitude, and the assurance of my lasting love?

By engaging with these questions, you can cultivate open, honest family conversations, clarify your final wishes, and nurture a sense of shared understanding. This reflective process encourages the healing of old wounds, the appreciation of mutual support, and the transmission of cherished values—guiding the family toward greater unity, strength, and peace as they carry forward the family legacy into the next chapter of life's unfolding story.

3.3. **Friendship and Community Support**: Connecting with close friends, spiritual communities, or support groups for emotional bolstering and guidance.

Below is a set of reflective, introspective questions centered on the theme of **"Friend**ship and Community Support." These questions are designed to encourage you approaching the end of life to delve deeply into your personal histories, current relationships, spiritual values, and ultimate quest for meaning. By engaging with these prompts, you may discover renewed emotional strength, resolve lingering conflicts, and find comfort and guidance through your connections with friends, community members, and supportive spiritual groups.

a. Revisiting Personal Histories and Community Roots

Reflecting on Past Friendships and Influences

- Which friendships throughout my life have provided the most support, understanding, or inspiration?
- What moments can I recall when close friends, mentors, or community members helped me through challenging times, and how might reflecting on these memories bring me comfort now?How have various communities—spiritual congregations, neighborhood groups, cultural associations—shaped my sense of belonging and identity?

Learning from Past Social Connections

- In what ways did my involvement in group activities—choirs, study circles, charitable efforts—enrich my spiritual and emotional life?
- When did I hesitate to seek help from my community or friends in the past, and what lessons can I draw from that reluctance as I reflect now?
- How have I shared my gifts—such as wisdom, time, or kindness—with my community, and how might recalling these contributions affirm my personal worth and legacy?

b. Assessing Current Support Networks and Emotional Needs

Identifying Sources of Strength and Comfort

- Which friends or spiritual companions bring me calm, understanding, or a sense of safety as I face the unknown?
- What support groups—such as bereavement circles, faith-based gatherings, or wellness communities—might provide me with guidance and a shared sense of purpose as I near life's end?How does the presence of loyal friends, prayer partners, or trusted advisors alleviate my fears and ease emotional burdens?

Clarifying Communication and Boundaries

- What do I need most from my friends and community at this stage—listening ears, practical help, spiritual counsel, or simply companionship?

What areas of my life or feelings have I hesitated to share, and how might opening up now deepen my sense of connection and understanding?How can I set aside pride or fear of imposing to request what I genuinely need, trusting that true friends and communities will understand and support my vulnerabilities?

c. Navigating Unfulfilled Goals, Unresolved Conflicts, and Evolving Relationships

Addressing Lingering Tensions

- What friendships that ended on uncertain terms or community relationships strained by misunderstanding might I now seek to heal or find closure with?How could honest conversations, letters, or prayers of reconciliation help mend unresolved conflicts and bring peace to both my heart and theirs?How can acknowledging shared human frailty—our fears, insecurities, and regrets—dissolve old resentments and foster mutual understanding?

Accepting Imperfections and Embracing Forgiveness

What regrets do I hold about not investing more time or openness in certain friendships or community ties, and how might I address them?How can I forgive myself and others for missed opportunities, trusting that our intentions and care still hold value?How might releasing perfectionism—expectations that friendships or communities should have offered more or been different—help me appreciate what we have shared?

d. Seeking Spiritual Meaning, Comfort, and Reconciliation in Community

Finding Spiritual Anchors Through Others

- How can the presence of supportive friends and spiritual companions help me affirm my beliefs, find spiritual resonance, or experience a greater sense of the divine?
- What communal rituals—such as group prayers, meditations, chanting, or singing—bring me closer to an experience of sacred connection and uplift my spirit?In what ways does the compassionate witness of others remind me that I am part of a greater tapestry of love, faith, and purpose?

Connecting with Collective Wisdom and Legacy

- What spiritual or moral insights have I gleaned from observing how others in my community face adversity, grief, or mortality?

How can I find comfort in knowing that my struggles and doubts are not unique, and that many before and after me have leaned on community support to find their way? How might reflecting on the cycles of communal life—such as births, traditions, and commemorations—help me view my own journey as part of an ongoing, meaningful narrative?

e. **Crafting a Meaningful Closing Chapter with the Help of Friends and Community**

Planning Conversations and Expressions of Gratitude

- What friendships do I wish to honor by openly expressing gratitude and love, ensuring no kind word remains unsaid?
- How can I arrange a gathering—physical or virtual—to share stories, memories, or blessings that strengthen our mutual bonds and reassure everyone of our lasting connections?
- How might writing letters, recording messages, or offering small tokens of appreciation extend my presence into the future and comfort those who remain?

Leaving a Legacy of Compassion and Understanding

- How can I encourage my friends and community members to continue supporting each other, learning from my experiences, and building upon the connections we've formed?
- How can sharing my beliefs, lessons learned, or spiritual convictions inspire others to cultivate empathy, faith, or resilience in their own lives?
- How might acknowledging the communal nature of our human journey—our need to lean on and learn from each other—help me face death with peace, knowing that the love we've nurtured endures?

f. **Embracing the Ongoing Presence of Friendship and Community Support**

Trusting in Enduring Bonds

- How can I find solace in the idea that the love and support I've given and received through friendships and community ties will live on in the hearts and actions of others?
- What spiritual or faith traditions teach that those who have gone before remain in communion with the living, offering comfort and guidance across unseen boundaries?
- How does trusting in the continuity of human connection—believing that we remain part of each other's stories—lighten my fears and bring me hope?

Surrendering to the Strength of Collective Love

- How might recognizing that I am carried on a wave of collective kindness and communal care help me let go of fear, isolation, or doubt?
- How can I surrender to this network of support, confident that my soul's journey is held in the gentle embrace of friends, faith communities, and the greater human family?
- How does accepting that my life touched and was touched by others bring me profound reassurance that my essence and influence persist through relationships and shared memory?

By contemplating these questions, you can approach the end of life with greater clarity, emotional security, and spiritual insight. Exploring past connections, current support systems, unresolved tensions, and the broader meaning of communal love encourages an environment where friendships and spiritual communities serve as pillars of strength. Ultimately, this reflective process reveals that you are not alone, and that the networks you've woven—through kindness, faith, and understanding—remain vital and life-affirming, even in the face of mortality.

3.4. **Legacy in the Lives of Others**: Considering how one's life story will live on in children, grandchildren, mentees, or the broader community.

Below is a set of reflective, introspective questions focused on the theme of "Legacy in the Lives of Others." These questions invite you nearing the end of life to deeply consider how your values, experiences, relationships, and teachings will continue to influence children, grandchildren, mentees, and the broader community. By contemplating these questions, you can foster spiritual and emotional growth, work toward reconciliation with unfulfilled goals or unresolved conflicts, and find enduring meaning in the legacy you leave behind.

a. **Personal Experiences and Memories: Identifying the Core of One's Legacy**

Recognizing Pivotal Life Lessons

- What defining moments—struggles, triumphs, epiphanies—shaped the person I've become, and how might sharing these lessons guide others after I am gone?
- What values or principles—such as integrity, compassion, or perseverance—have I consistently lived by, and how might they serve as guiding lights for future generations?
- Which stories from my past, whether joyful or challenging, contain wisdom that could help my descendants or community members navigate their own journeys?

Examining Personal Growth and Transformation

- What instances of growing from adversity can I recall, where I transcended hardship into greater understanding, and how might sharing these insights benefit those who follow?
- In what ways have my spiritual beliefs or moral convictions matured over time, and how can I communicate this spiritual evolution to others seeking direction?
- How can I view my life as a narrative of continuous learning, framing both my successes and failures as valuable "map points" for others traveling similar paths?

b. **Relationships and Interpersonal Connections: Sharing Love, Guidance, and Example**

Influencing Close Family Members

- How have I impacted my children, grandchildren, or other close relatives through my actions, words, and presence? Which qualities would I most like them to carry forward?
- What traditions or rituals—such as holiday customs, family meals, or storytelling sessions—do I hope will persist to connect future generations to our shared heritage?
- How can I take time to express love, gratitude, or encouragement to younger family members, ensuring they know their worth and potential?

Supporting Mentees and Community Members

- In what ways have I mentored or supported others outside my immediate family—students, colleagues, neighbors—and how can I affirm the significance of these contributions?
- Is there advice, professional insight, or moral guidance I offered that might continue to resonate with those I've helped, shaping their choices and character?
- How might the example of my dedication, work ethic, or compassion inspire others to contribute positively to their communities?

c. **Unfulfilled Goals, Unresolved Conflicts, and Finding Closure for the Sake of Legacy**

Addressing Lingering Aspirations

- What dreams or goals did I not accomplish, and how can I find meaning in the attempts, lessons learned, or the inspiration they might offer to others?

- How can I accept that leaving some ambitions unrealized does not diminish my legacy but instead enriches it with authenticity and human vulnerability?
- How might acknowledging these incomplete chapters show future generations that it's possible to find worth in striving, not just in achieving?

Revisiting Conflicts and Forgiveness

- What unresolved tensions or conflicts could I address through apologies or understanding to leave a cleaner, more compassionate legacy for those who follow?
- How can I communicate forgiveness or understanding—either spoken or written—to ensure my legacy is not burdened by bitterness or regret?
- How does making peace with past misunderstandings demonstrate to others that healing and reconciliation are always within reach, even late in life?

d. The Search for Meaning, Reconciliation, and Spiritual Continuity

Aligning Legacy with Spiritual Beliefs

- How does my spiritual perspective (faith in the divine, belief in eternal values, reverence for the human spirit) inform the legacy I hope to leave behind?
- How can I express the spiritual truths or insights that sustained me, offering them as a beacon of comfort or direction for those seeking deeper meaning after my departure?
- In what ways can I highlight that the love and virtues we cultivate transcend physical life, suggesting that my presence continues spiritually in the hearts of others?

Embracing Moral and Ethical Dimensions

- How do I see my life's impact extending beyond material accomplishments to include moral influences, ethical decisions, and compassionate deeds that ripple forward?
- How can I reassure my loved ones that even small acts of kindness or honesty carry lasting significance, reinforcing shared values for generations to come?
- How can I frame my legacy as an ongoing moral conversation, inviting others to refine, reinterpret, and elevate the principles I tried to embody?

e. **Practical Expressions of Legacy: Ensuring Continuity and Remembrance**

Creating Tangible Reminders

- What letters, memoirs, recordings, or creative works can I leave behind to convey my experiences, beliefs, and heartfelt messages directly to future recipients?
- How might curating photographs, heirlooms, or keepsakes that narrate my journey connect my loved ones to a tangible past and encourage them to preserve their own narratives?
- How can my will, ethical testament, or spiritual final words provide clarity, stability, or guidance, ensuring that my legacy remains accessible and comprehensible?

Fostering a Culture of Storytelling and Reflection

- How can I encourage my family, friends, and community to gather regularly—through reunions, commemorations, or shared rituals—to keep our collective history alive?
- How can openly discussing my life's lessons and regrets inspire others to engage more thoughtfully in their own growth and contributions?
- In what ways can I nurture a lasting dialogue—between the past, present, and future—that sustains communal wisdom and moral continuity?

f. **Integrating Legacy into the Final Chapter: Embracing Peace, Fulfillment, and Hope**

Accepting the Impermanence and Continuity of Life

- How can I find solace in knowing that my essence endures not only through memory but also through the values, kindness, and understandings I've passed on?
- How does acknowledging that each generation builds upon the last, evolving and refining the legacy, provide me with comfort and a sense of cosmic harmony?
- What helps me release fear and anxiety, trusting that what I've shared—my character, my principles, and my love—will continue to bear fruit beyond my physical lifespan?

Completing the Circle of Life and Legacy

- How might embracing the natural cycle of birth, life, death, and renewal help me see my legacy as part of a larger tapestry of human endeavor?

- How can I envision my role as one link in a chain of ancestors and descendants, each contributing unique insights and strengthening the collective spirit?
- How might offering my final blessings help me rest in the knowledge that my life has mattered, that I have influenced others, and that my story will guide them along their own paths?

By reflecting on these questions, you approaching the end of life may gain a fuller understanding of your legacy's impact. Acknowledging personal growth, transmitting ethical and spiritual principles, and reconciling unfulfilled goals or unresolved conflicts can guide you to a place of inner peace. Ultimately, these contemplations affirm that your life story will live on, inspiring future generations to embrace kindness, resilience, and meaningful living.

3.5. **Cultural and Social Identity**: Reflecting on how cultural traditions, social norms, and community values shape end-of-life rituals and personal identity at life's end.

Below is a list of reflective and introspective questions centered on the theme of "Cultural and Social Identity." These questions invite you approaching the end of life to explore how cultural traditions, social norms, and community values have shaped your end-of-life perspectives, personal identity, and spiritual understanding. Each subcategory aims to guide you toward greater clarity, reconciliation, and spiritual growth by examining your past experiences, present relationships, unfinished business, and the search for meaning within the cultural tapestry of your live.

a. **Personal Experiences and Memories: Unearthing Cultural Roots and Influences**

Cultural Traditions and Early Impressions

- What cultural traditions were most present during my upbringing, and how did they inform my understanding of life, death, and the afterlife?
- What specific customs, stories, or rites of passage have taught me what it means to live honorably and die with dignity within my cultural context?
- Which childhood memories—festivals, family gatherings, religious ceremonies—have most shaped the way I perceive end-of-life rituals?

Evolving Sense of Self Within a Cultural Framework

- How have I embraced or challenged my cultural heritage at different points in my life, and how has this shaped my identity as I approach my final chapter?

- In what ways have my travels, education, or exposure to other cultures broadened or refined my perspective on dying and what constitutes a meaningful farewell?
- What moments can I identify where I consciously integrated cultural values—such as respect for elders, community solidarity, or spiritual devotion—into my worldview, and how have these influenced my final wishes?

b. Relationships and Interpersonal Connections: Community Values and Social Bonds

Influence of Family and Community

- How have my family's cultural beliefs and practices influenced my approach to mortality, including rituals of remembrance and mourning?
- Which community elders, religious leaders, or mentors embodied cultural ideals, and how might their guidance and example bring me comfort now?
- How do the communal aspects of my heritage—such as shared meals, communal prayer, traditional music, or dance—strengthen my sense of belonging and ease my fears about dying?

Communicating Cultural Wishes to Loved Ones

- How can I clearly express to my family or close friends the cultural traditions or spiritual rites I wish to be honored at my passing?
- How might inviting loved ones to participate in culturally meaningful rituals—chanting, storytelling, lighting incense, wearing traditional attire—promote understanding and closeness at life's end?
- What steps can I take to explain the symbolic meaning behind certain cultural practices, helping my loved ones carry these traditions forward and find solace in them after I am gone?

c. Unfulfilled Goals, Unresolved Conflicts, and Cultural Expectations

Reconciling Cultural Expectations with Personal Desires

- What cultural or social expectations—such as family roles, community responsibilities, or rituals—did I never fulfill, and how might this leave me feeling incomplete or conflicted?
- How can I find acceptance in acknowledging that not all cultural ideals align perfectly with my personal journey, and that my worth is not solely defined by adherence to tradition?

- How might I forgive myself and others for any tension or disappointment arising from unmet cultural norms, recognizing that human lives often transcend neat cultural boundaries?

Transforming Regret into Cultural Understanding

- What cultural skills—such as language, art forms, or spiritual practices—do I regret not passing on to younger generations, and how can I offer these teachings now, even symbolically?
- How might openly discussing the meaning and importance of cultural traditions help heal conflicts caused by misunderstandings in my relationships before it is too late?
- How can I redefine my legacy, focusing not on what was left undone but on the sincerity of my efforts to live authentically within my cultural framework?

d. The Search for Meaning, Reconciliation, and Spiritual Integration

Aligning Cultural Identity with Spiritual Beliefs

- How do my cultural traditions intersect with or differ from my spiritual or religious beliefs about life and death?
- How can I reconcile contradictions between inherited cultural norms and my personal spiritual convictions to find a balanced understanding that brings me peace?
- In what ways might embracing the universal themes of compassion, love, forgiveness, and unity within my culture's narrative soothe my soul and guide me toward reconciliation?

Embracing Diversity and Universal Wisdom

- What insights have I drawn from other cultures that highlight universal human themes—such as honor, remembrance, and gratitude—and how do they resonate with me?
- How can acknowledging the multiplicity of cultural approaches to understanding mortality help me see my journey as part of a global human story rather than feeling isolated by my unique background?
- How does embracing the wisdom of various traditions—through prayer, meditation, sacred music, or storytelling—offer me comfort and broaden my spiritual horizons?

e. Practical Considerations and Ritual Expressions at Life's End

Crafting a Culturally Meaningful Farewell

- Which rituals, ceremonies, or symbolic acts do I wish to incorporate into my end-of-life observances to honor my cultural roots—special hymns, traditional attire, offerings to ancestors, community gatherings?
- How can I communicate my preferences for funeral or memorial arrangements that reflect my cultural identity, ensuring those who remain understand the significance of these choices?
- How can I explain the relevance of integrating practices from different cultures I've encountered, so my loved ones can unite these elements meaningfully?

Guiding Future Generations

- In what ways can I encourage younger family members or community members to keep certain traditions alive, adapting them thoughtfully for future contexts?
- How might I use letters, recorded messages, or written reflections to transmit cultural wisdom and spiritual insights, leaving a guide for others navigating their own end-of-life journeys?
- How can I express trust that evolving cultural practices will continue to preserve the essence of what mattered to me, even as they transform over time?

f. Embracing Peace and Belonging in One's Cultural and Spiritual Identity

Finding Comfort in Cultural Belonging

- How can recognizing that my cultural and social identity anchors me in a long lineage of human experience, connecting me to ancestors and future descendants, bring me a deep sense of peace?
- How does affirming my cultural heritage quell fears of isolation or insignificance, assuring me that I am part of a larger tapestry that transcends individual mortality?
- How does acknowledging the enduring communal memory—passed down through songs, stories, and moral teachings—help me feel that my essence will continue in the collective spirit rather than vanish?

Achieving Inner Harmony at Life's Threshold

- How can reconciling cultural traditions with personal beliefs help me rest in the certainty that I have lived a life shaped by meaningful values, guided by faith, and enriched by community support?
- How does finding spiritual comfort in the idea that my cultural identity, while distinct, is woven into a universal human narrative of love, learning, and transcendence ease my journey?

- How might embracing my cultural roots and integrating them with my inner spiritual compass allow me to approach my final moments with gratitude, acceptance, and profound inner calm?

Engaging with these questions encourages you to understand how cultural traditions, social norms, and community values inform your identity and end-of-life choices. It paves the way for deeper reconciliation, stronger connections with loved ones, and a gentler acceptance of mortality. Ultimately, this reflective process affirms that cultural identity—far from being a mere backdrop—shapes the very manner in which you approach your final passages, illuminating your path with shared meaning, memory, and spiritual resonance.

Chapter 4. Physical and Medical Factors

4.1. **Pain Management and Comfort**: Working with caregivers and medical professionals to ensure as much physical comfort as possible.

Below is a collection of reflective and introspective questions centered on the theme of "Pain Management and Comfort." These questions are designed to help you approaching the end of life consider how to best ensure your physical comfort in collaboration with caregivers and medical professionals, while also reflecting deeply on personal history, relationships, unresolved desires, and the search for meaning. Each subcategory encourages self-exploration, ultimately guiding you toward a sense of ease, acceptance, and spiritual resonance as you face mortality.

a. **Personal Experiences and Memories: Understanding One's Relationship with the Body and Pain**

Awareness of Body and Self-Care History

- How have I tended to my body's needs throughout my life—through exercise, rest, nourishment, and medical attention?
- What past experiences of pain, injury, or illness have taught me to communicate more effectively with caregivers or advocate for my comfort?
- In reflecting on how I managed discomfort before, what eased my suffering—such as spiritual practices, certain environments, reassuring words, or touch—and how can I apply this now?

Accepting Changing Limitations

- How have I learned to accept the gradual changes in my body as I aged or became ill?

- How can I make peace with needing assistance, trusting that asking for help does not diminish my dignity or worth?
- What feelings arise when I acknowledge that my physical capabilities have shifted, and how can recognizing this truth guide me toward compassion for myself?

Honoring the Body's Sacredness

- How can I view my body as a sacred vessel that has carried me through life's experiences, even as it now experiences pain?
- How might honoring my body's history—its strengths and vulnerabilities—help me appreciate the importance of seeking comfort in my final days?
- In what ways can I integrate spiritual or religious rituals (anointing, prayer, meditation) to bring solace to my physical discomfort?

b. **Relationships and Interpersonal Connections: Involving Caregivers and Loved Ones in the Journey Toward Comfort**

Communicating Needs and Boundaries

- How can I clearly express my pain levels, fears, and preferences to caregivers, family members, and medical professionals?
- Who among my loved ones do I trust to advocate on my behalf if I become unable to speak for myself, ensuring that my comfort remains a priority?
- How can I create an environment of openness, where my caregivers feel welcomed to ask questions and I feel safe to respond honestly?

Receiving Compassion and Support

- How do I feel about relying on others for basic comfort measures, such as adjusting pillows, controlling room temperature, or providing gentle touch and reassurance?
- How can I allow myself to receive care as an act of love rather than perceiving it as a burden on those around me?
- How can I show gratitude to my caregivers and family, acknowledging their efforts and compassion, even during moments of discomfort or frustration?

Maintaining Emotional Connection

- How can the presence of loved ones—through conversation, shared memories, or spiritual reading—help alleviate both physical and emotional pain?

- How might involving spiritual advisors, chaplains, or religious community members to pray with me or offer rituals bring me comfort and soothe my soul as I face pain?
- What meaningful objects, photographs, music, or scents can I incorporate to remind me of loved ones and enhance my sense of comfort and security?

c. Unfulfilled Goals, Unresolved Conflicts, and Their Impact on Comfort

Inner Tensions and Pain Perception

- How can expressing appreciation to those who have supported me lighten my heart and create moments of shared solace?
- What steps can I take—even now—to mend relationships, seek forgiveness, or grant it, to ease inner turmoil that may magnify my pain?
- How can I confront the emotional weight of unfulfilled dreams, aspirations, or roles I have not fully realized, and allow acceptance of this truth to bring spiritual relief?

Releasing Regret and Finding Acceptance

- What tension or resentment do I carry related to past medical decisions, personal choices, or unmet expectations regarding my health, and how can I address it?
- How can forgiveness—of myself and others—serve as a form of spiritual analgesic, softening the edges of physical pain with understanding and compassion?
- How might letting go of struggles over what I could not control bring a sense of calming relief and translate into greater physical comfort?

Balancing Emotional and Physical Care

- How have I communicated to my caregivers that managing my discomfort involves not only medication or physical interventions but also the need to feel understood, respected, and heard?
- How could addressing deeper emotional wounds—through heartfelt conversations, letter writing, or spiritual counsel—help lessen the burden my body carries?

d. The Search for Meaning, Reconciliation, and Spiritual Peace in Pain Management

Embracing the Purpose Behind Care

- How can I view medical treatments, palliative measures, and attention from caregivers as manifestations of love and compassion rather than mere clinical interventions?
- How might trusting the expertise and goodwill of those who care for me reflect my faith in a benevolent universe or a guiding spiritual presence?
- How might I interpret the act of seeking comfort as part of my spiritual journey, teaching me patience, humility, and grace?

Integrating Spiritual Practices for Comfort

- What spiritual practices can I incorporate to help me cope with physical pain—mindful breathing, prayer, visualization, or religious sacraments—that might bring calmness to both body and soul?
- What mantra, scripture passage, sacred image, or hymn offers me a sense of refuge and helps reduce my experience of pain or fear?
- How can I find significance in offering my discomfort to a higher power, trusting that my suffering might serve a mysterious spiritual purpose or deepen my empathy for others?

Finding Meaning in Vulnerability

- How can acknowledging my vulnerability help me understand that life's worth is not measured by physical strength alone, but by the depth of my spirit and the love I share with others?
- How might facing pain at the end of life help me appreciate the gift of existence, reaffirming my connection to the divine and to all living beings who also experience suffering and transcendence?
- How might releasing my hold on physical control bring comfort through the belief that I am cared for—by people, by faith, or by the cosmos—and that I am never truly alone?

e. **Integration and Conclusion: Crafting a Holistic Vision of Comfort and Peace**

Evaluating Personal Priorities

- How can understanding the interplay between my emotional state, spiritual beliefs, and physical condition guide decisions about pain management strategies (e.g., medication levels, complementary therapies)?
- In what ways can I balance the desire for a clear mind with the need for pain relief, aligning medical choices with my spiritual values and personal dignity?

Leaving a Legacy of Compassionate Care

- How might my approach to pain management become a lesson for loved ones, showing them the importance of advocating for their comfort and well-being?
- How can seeking comfort and relief reassure me that I am inspiring others to treat themselves and each other with gentleness and understanding?

Surrendering into Peace

- How can I surrender any remaining struggle against discomfort in this final stage, trusting that everything has been done to ensure my ease and that I am held in compassion and care?
- How does embracing the support and relief offered to me help me feel prepared—physically, emotionally, and spiritually—to face the mystery of what lies beyond this life?

By contemplating these questions, you are encouraged to forge a deeper connection between your physical comfort, emotional well-being, and spiritual perspective. This reflective process can bring solace, guiding you toward a more peaceful and meaningful relationship with your body, your caregivers, and the sacred journey toward life's end.

4.2. **Palliative and Hospice Care Options**: Understanding care models designed to support dignity, comfort, and quality of life rather than cure.

Below is a collection of reflective and introspective questions centered on the theme of "Palliative and Hospice Care Options." These questions guide you to consider the role of these care models—focused on dignity, comfort, and quality of life rather than cure—in the context of your personal histories, relationships, unmet aspirations, and spiritual longings. By inviting deep reflection, these questions aim to foster acceptance, healing, and inner peace as you navigate the complexities of approaching the end of life.

a. **Personal Experiences and Memories: Honoring the Life Lived**

Reflecting on Past Encounters with Care and Support

- When I think about times I received care in the past—whether during illness, injury, or emotional hardship—what was most comforting or reassuring to me?
- What moments have I experienced when someone cared for me in a way that preserved my dignity and sense of self, and what can I learn from those memories as I consider hospice or palliative care now?
- How have past medical treatments or hospital stays influenced my understanding of what compassionate care should look like at life's end?

Embracing the Present Moment

- How can I shift my perspective from "fixing" or "fighting" illness to embracing care that respects my current reality, focusing on comfort and quality of life?
- What aspects of my day-to-day experience—such as enjoying natural light, comforting scents, gentle music, or quiet prayer—might hospice or palliative care teams help me preserve or enhance?

Finding Meaning in Care Choices

- How can choosing a palliative or hospice approach honor the whole person I have become over time, rather than only addressing the part of me that is ill?
- How can I see these care models as a reflection of the values I've held throughout my life—kindness, presence, and patience—now being directed toward myself?

b.   Relationships and Interpersonal Connections: Communication, Trust, and Mutual Support

Inviting Loved Ones into the Decision

- How do I feel about discussing hospice or palliative care options with my family and friends?
- How can I share my wishes openly while listening to my loved ones' feelings and concerns, so that we can find a path that respects everyone's emotional well-being?
- What helps me trust that involving loved ones in these decisions will bring us closer, allowing them to support me in a way that honors my dignity and comfort?

Nurturing Bonds Through Compassionate Care

- In what ways might palliative or hospice care settings foster deeper connections with those I love—through heartfelt conversations, shared memories, or spiritual rituals?
- How can I view the caregiving team as an extension of my circle of support, helping me and my loved ones navigate this tender time with understanding and empathy?

Strengthening Relationships in Vulnerability

- How might the vulnerability I feel at this stage of life open opportunities for reconciliation, forgiveness, or unspoken gratitude within my closest relationships?

- How can I accept help from others—family, friends, or professionals—without shame or regret, recognizing that receiving care can be as meaningful as giving it?

c. Unfulfilled Goals, Unresolved Conflicts, and Their Influence on Care Decisions

Reassessing Life Priorities

- Are there lingering goals I can no longer pursue as I once intended, and how can focusing on comfort, dignity, and emotional well-being help me make peace with these limitations?
- How can accepting palliative or hospice care help me redirect my energy from striving toward achievements to cherishing the legacy I've already created?

Addressing Internal and External Tensions

- How do unresolved conflicts—whether with family, friends, or within myself—contribute to stress that might intensify my physical or emotional suffering?
- How can I involve hospice or palliative care professionals, chaplains, or counselors in facilitating conversations or inner work that ease these tensions, thus improving my quality of life?

Forgiveness and Release

- How can acknowledging that life's remaining chapter is about comfort and presence rather than control or cure help me more readily forgive myself and others for what remains undone?
- How does focusing on comfort, rather than cure, prompt me to let go of resentments or disappointments, opening space for peace and understanding?

d. The Search for Meaning, Reconciliation, and Spiritual Growth

Reframing the End of Life as Sacred Time

- How can choosing hospice or palliative care help me embrace this stage of life as a meaningful transition, rather than a mere conclusion?
- How can I interpret the focus on comfort and dignity as part of a divine or universal plan, inviting me to rest, reflect, and spiritually prepare?

Deepening Spiritual Insight

- Which spiritual practices—prayer, meditation, sacred readings, or quiet reflection—might I integrate into this care journey, and how can they guide me toward inner peace and acceptance?
- How can I view the limitations imposed by illness as pathways to deeper compassion, understanding, or unity with the divine, rather than as losses?

Connecting Care Choices to a Broader Spiritual Narrative

- In what ways does acknowledging that cure may no longer be the goal align with spiritual teachings about impermanence, surrender, and the sanctity of the soul's journey?
- How can embracing palliative or hospice care strengthen my faith or spiritual conviction, affirming that I am held in love and care—both human and divine—in my final days?

e. Integration and Acceptance: Embracing a Holistic Approach to Care

Balancing Body, Mind, and Spirit

- How can I ensure that my care plan addresses not just my physical symptoms, but also my emotional well-being and spiritual longings?
- What complementary therapies—such as music therapy, massage, chaplain visits, or art therapy—might enhance my comfort and dignity, reflecting the fullness of who I am?

Legacy and Continuity

- How can knowing that choosing palliative or hospice care demonstrates the values of compassion and acceptance I hope to pass on to those I love bring me comfort?
- How might this choice become part of my legacy—showing future generations that embracing comfort, openness, and spiritual readiness at life's end is an act of courage and grace?

Embracing the Unknown with Support

- How can I trust that, as I approach this threshold, the professionals and loved ones at my side will help me navigate pain, fear, and uncertainty with empathy and skill?
- How might surrendering to the care offered bring me solace, knowing that I am not alone and that the path ahead is softened by understanding and love?

By contemplating these questions, you may find that understanding and embracing palliative or hospice care options can transform the experience of dying into a sacred, meaningful time. Engaging with personal memories, healing relationships, making peace with unfulfilled goals, and seeking spiritual depth can help ensure that the journey remains guided by dignity, comfort, and the unwavering presence of compassion.

4.3. **Symptom Control and Quality of Life**: Balancing treatments, medications, and interventions that align with one's values and goals.

Below is a set of reflective and introspective questions centered on the theme of "Symptom Control and Quality of Life." These questions are designed to help you consider how to balance treatments, medications, and interventions with your deeper values, personal history, relationships, regrets, and spiritual understanding. They encourage looking inward to determine how best to approach physical comfort while preserving spiritual integrity and emotional peace.

a. **Personal Experiences and Memories: Reassessing Health Journeys and Body Awareness**

Reflecting on Past Health Decisions

- When have I felt most in tune with my body—aware of its strengths, its vulnerabilities, and its needs?
- What past instances of making important medical choices can I recall, and how might the principles that guided me then support me now?
- What treatments or interventions from the past felt more burdensome than beneficial, and what insights do these experiences offer me today?

Valuing Comfort and Well-Being

- At this stage of life, what do I cherish most in my daily experience—clear thinking, relief from pain, the ability to enjoy simple pleasures—and how can I prioritize this in my treatment plan?
- How might past experiences with pain or discomfort inform my understanding of what is an acceptable trade-off between relief and potential side effects of medications?

Honoring the Body's Story

- If I view my body as a sacred vessel that has carried me through life, how can I align treatments with a spirit of reverence and compassion toward myself?
- Have I taken the time to acknowledge the journey my body has been on—the trials, recoveries, and adaptations—and how can this recognition guide my current health decisions?

b. Relationships and Interpersonal Connections: Communicating Needs and Inviting Understanding

Open Dialogue with Loved Ones

- How can I clearly communicate my treatment preferences to those who care for me, ensuring that they understand my reasons and support my choices?
- How can I encourage honest, loving conversations with family and friends about balancing symptom management with maintaining my quality of life?
- What helps me trust my loved ones or designated healthcare proxies to advocate for my comfort and uphold my values if I become unable to speak for myself?

Relying on Professional Expertise

- How can I seek the counsel of compassionate doctors, nurses, and care teams who understand and support my physical, emotional, and spiritual priorities?
- How can I find practitioners who respect my autonomy, listen deeply, and help me tailor interventions that fit my value system rather than imposing a one-size-fits-all approach?

Fostering Mutual Understanding

- How might involving spiritual advisors, chaplains, or faith leaders in discussions about symptom control help ensure that my approach aligns with both my medical and spiritual frameworks?
- How can honest communication about my goals—such as maintaining mental clarity for final conversations or minimizing pain to experience peace—foster deeper understanding and connection with those around me?

c. Unfulfilled Goals, Unresolved Conflicts, and the Impact on Quality of Life Decisions

Weighing Life's Priorities Amid Limitations

- What aspirations do I now recognize as unattainable, and how can acknowledging these limitations guide my decisions toward comfort and inner peace?
- How can focusing on what I can still enjoy—time with loved ones, meaningful conversations, and spiritual practices—help me accept certain treatments or reject others?

Releasing Regret and Guilt

- How might holding onto regret or guilt affect how I perceive my self-worth and influence my health decisions?
- If unresolved conflicts make symptom control feel like a last resort or a "giving up," how can I reframe this perspective to see it as a courageous acceptance of life as it is?

Healing Inner Turmoil

- How might addressing emotional pain—through forgiveness, apologies, or honest reflection—help lessen the intensity of my physical discomfort?
- What non-physical "symptoms," such as fear, anxiety, or anger, deserve attention to improve my overall quality of life, even if all physical symptoms cannot be fully relieved?

d. **The Search for Meaning and Reconciliation: Aligning Treatments with Spiritual and Ethical Values**

Defining a Spiritually Aligned Approach

- How does my faith or spiritual understanding inform my view of medical interventions—do I see them as gifts, tests of faith, or opportunities for surrender?
- How can I reconcile the desire to minimize suffering with the understanding that some discomfort may hold meaning within my spiritual journey?

Embracing the Present Moment

- What does quality of life mean to me spiritually—quiet contemplation, the ability to pray, to express gratitude, to savor moments with loved ones?
- How can I ensure that my treatment choices enhance my capacity to remain present, aware, and attuned to the sacredness of each remaining moment?

Balancing Acceptance and Effort

- How can I accept the limits of medicine, acknowledging that not all pain can be erased, while remaining open to measures that enhance comfort and tranquility?
- How might focusing on inner peace, rather than solely on symptom elimination, provide a sense of spiritual equilibrium?

Confronting Mortality with Grace

- How can my treatment choices help me face mortality with dignity, understanding, and a sense of sacred passage rather than dread?
- How does recognizing the finite nature of life influence my willingness to simplify or reduce interventions that may prolong life but diminish its quality?

e. Integration and Acceptance: Crafting a Holistic Path to Wholeness

Harmonizing Body, Mind, and Soul

- How can balancing symptom control with my personal values help me weave together the physical, emotional, and spiritual aspects of my being into a coherent whole?
- What complementary therapies—massage, music, art, spiritual counsel—could enhance my quality of life, supporting not just my body, but my heart and soul?

Leaving a Meaningful Legacy

- How does choosing certain treatments or rejecting others reflect a final lesson or legacy I wish to leave behind, such as courage, authenticity, or trust in the divine?
- How can the thought that my approach to care will guide my loved ones to value quality of life and personal dignity bring me comfort as they face their own health challenges?

Surrendering into Inner Peace

- How can acknowledging my physical limits free me from unrealistic expectations, allowing me to find strength in vulnerability and trust in the care provided?
- How can settling on a strategy for managing symptoms help me release anxiety over what I cannot change and allow me to rest peacefully in the knowledge that I have chosen a path honoring my truest self?

By contemplating these questions, you can navigate the complex interplay between medical realities and deeply held values. This reflective process supports informed, compassionate decision-making that recognizes not only the body's needs but also the heart's longings and the soul's innate desire for meaning and peace. Each question invites a holistic integration of body, mind, and spirit, guiding individuals toward a path of dignity, comfort, and authenticity as you approach the end of life.

4.4. **Personal Autonomy in Treatment Decisions**: Asserting preferences regarding life-sustaining measures, resuscitation, feeding tubes, or ventilators.

Below is a collection of introspective questions focused on "Personal Autonomy in Treatment Decisions." These questions are designed to help you clarify your values, fears, and hopes about life-sustaining measures such as resuscitation, feeding tubes, or ventilators as you approach the end of life. The questions delve into personal history, relationships, unfulfilled goals, spiritual understanding, and the quest for meaning. They encourage deep reflection and are organized into thematic subcategories to foster clarity, growth, and inner peace.

a. **Personal Experiences and Memories: Reflecting on One's Health Journey**

Revisiting Past Encounters with Medical Treatment

- What past experiences with illness, surgery, or hospitalization have shaped my understanding of what it means to be cared for medically?
- Have I witnessed friends or family members facing end-of-life treatment decisions? What did I learn from their choices or experiences?
- What moments can I recall when medical interventions either enhanced my sense of dignity or made me feel reduced to just a patient rather than a whole person?

Assessing Pain, Comfort, and Quality of Life

- What are my earliest memories of pain or physical struggle, and how did I cope with them?
- How do I prioritize maintaining alertness and comfort over extending life through invasive measures, and what factors influence my willingness to accept certain interventions in pursuit of longevity?
- When I imagine the last days of my life, what sensations—light, warmth, familiar voices—matter most to me, and how might certain treatments support or impede these experiences?

Embodying Personal Values

- Which personal values have guided my life decisions, and how do they apply to my medical choices now?
- How do I balance accepting limitations on mobility or communication to prolong life with my preference for a natural decline that preserves authenticity and agency?
- How would I describe a "good death" for myself, and what role does personal autonomy play in that vision?

b. **Relationships and Interpersonal Connections: Communicating Preferences and Honoring Bonds**

Sharing Wishes with Loved Ones

- Who are the people I trust to understand and respect my end-of-life decisions, and have I clearly communicated my preferences to them?
- How can I involve my closest companions, family members, or spiritual advisors in discussions about ventilators, feeding tubes, or resuscitation attempts?
- Do I fear that asserting my treatment choices might burden or upset those who love me, and if so, how can I address these concerns honestly and compassionately?

Balancing Individual Autonomy with Others' Emotions

- How can I find the courage to claim my right to self-determination in the face of loved ones who may yearn for me to prolong life at all costs?
- If my family's desires conflict with my own preferences, how can I navigate these differences while maintaining love and mutual respect?

Legacies of Understanding and Compassion

- How can I envision my loved ones finding solace and acceptance in knowing that the decisions I made were conscious and aligned with my core values?
- Will communicating my choices now help prevent future conflict, guilt, or confusion among those I leave behind, allowing them to remember me as someone who approached death thoughtfully and with integrity?

c. **Unfulfilled Goals, Unresolved Conflicts, and Reconciliation Through Medical Choices**

Accepting Limitations in Life's Final Chapter

- Are there unachieved goals or dreams that I must let go of, and how might this acceptance influence my readiness to forego aggressive interventions?
- How could acknowledging that my life is complete as it is—despite unfinished projects—ease the pressure to prolong life through artificial means?

Healing Through Honest Decisions

- What lingering emotional wounds or conflicts weigh on me, and how might making a clear decision about life support free me to focus on emotional healing rather than medical uncertainty?
- How can setting clear boundaries on what I am willing or unwilling to endure bring a sense of inner peace that helps resolve personal regrets or conflicts?

Finding Strength in Vulnerability

- How can embracing the vulnerability of this stage—acknowledging that not everything can be fixed—bring grace and clarity to my remaining relationships and self-understanding?
- If I accept the natural course of my body's decline, what opportunities arise for honest conversations, forgiveness, or heartfelt farewells that might not be possible if I am heavily sedated or reliant on machines?

d.   The Search for Meaning and Reconciliation: A Spiritual Lens on Treatment Choices

Aligning Choices with Spiritual or Religious Beliefs

- What do my faith traditions, spiritual practices, or religious texts say about the sanctity of life, the acceptance of mortality, and the use of medical technology at life's end?
- How do I view life-sustaining treatments—are they a way of honoring the gift of life, or do they feel like an interference with a divine plan or natural transition?

Embracing the Mystery of Mortality

- How can I find spiritual meaning in gradually letting go of physical existence, trusting that my soul's journey continues beyond the limits of the body?
- If I believe in an afterlife, divine presence, or universal spirit, how might surrendering to a natural death reflect trust in that greater mystery?

Finding Peace in Surrender

- How can relinquishing certain treatments become an act of faith, courage, or spiritual insight, rather than a failure or defeat?
- How can I view the decision to decline certain measures as a profound statement of acceptance that honors life's impermanence and invites a deeper connection with the sacred?

e.   Integration and Acceptance: Weaving Together Values, Relationships, and Spiritual Understanding

Holistic Decision-Making

- When considering feeding tubes, ventilators, or resuscitation, how can I integrate my physical comfort, emotional well-being, relational harmony, and spiritual peace into one coherent vision?
- What non-medical forms of support—such as prayer, music, nature, hand-holding, or storytelling—might I value more than life-sustaining interventions?

Leaving a Guiding Example

- How could my decisions about treatments serve as a guide or inspiration for others facing similar challenges, showing them that personal autonomy can coexist with love and compassion?

Final Affirmation of Self

- As I approach these decisions, how can I affirm the fullness of who I am—my personality, values, and faith—in the face of mortality?
- By taking ownership of my end-of-life choices, can I approach the threshold with serenity, gratitude, and a sense of integrity, knowing I have honored both myself and the sacredness of life's passage?

By contemplating these questions, you can navigate the deeply personal and profound territory of end-of-life medical choices with greater clarity and inner peace. This reflective process encourages honoring your past, communicating openly with loved ones, resolving unresolved matters, and discerning a spiritual perspective that infuses these decisions with significance. In doing so, you fosters a sense of autonomy that respects the human spirit's resilience, dignity, and sacred worth as life nears its conclusion.

4.5. **Planning for the Body's Transition**: Considering whether to donate organs; choose burial or cremation, or follow cultural/religious rites for the body.

Below is a set of introspective questions related to "Planning for the Body's Transition." Each category aims to guide you as you consider organ donation, burial or cremation, and cultural or religious rites. By addressing personal history, relationships, unfinished matters, and the search for meaning, these questions foster spiritual growth, emotional clarity, and a sense of wholeness. They are intended to help you approach this significant step with intention, honesty, and peace.

a.   Personal Experiences and Memories: Drawing Upon One's Life Story

Reflecting on Previous Encounters with Death and Ritual

- What funerals, memorials, or other rites have I attended that left a lasting impression on me, and how have they shaped my perspective?
- Which elements of those ceremonies resonated most deeply—ritual prayers, the presence of nature, music, certain readings, or the way the body was honored?

- If I think back to moments of personal loss, how did the handling of my loved ones' remains influence my grieving process?

Understanding Cultural and Familial Traditions

- Were there family traditions or cultural practices around death and the body's care that I witnessed growing up, and how did they shape my views today?
- What ancestral customs or family stories guide me toward a particular choice—such as burial near relatives, cremation, or organ donation as an act of legacy—and how do they influence my decisions?

Personal Comfort and Aesthetics

- What symbols or settings—such as a peaceful cemetery, an ocean scattering, or a quiet forest—bring me comfort and guide my decision for my body's final resting place?
- How might the sensory aspects of the chosen method (quiet prayers, incense, candlelight, natural surroundings) reflect the way I want to be remembered?

b. **Relationships and Interpersonal Connections: Honoring Bonds Through Final Arrangements**

Communicating with Loved Ones

- What conversations have I had—or do I need to have—with family and friends about my wishes for my body after death?
- How can I make my intentions clear, ensuring loved ones understand the meaning behind my choices and are prepared to uphold them?

Respecting the Feelings of Others

- How might my awareness of my loved ones' cultural or religious convictions influence my decisions, and how could these choices affect their sense of closure and comfort?
- How can I find room for compromise if family members find certain practices challenging, while still honoring my core values?

Creating a Space for Healing

- How might my chosen arrangements—be it organ donation, a specific funeral rite, or a particular resting place—offer solace, hope, or even inspiration to those I leave behind?
- How can my decision foster communal healing, such as through organ donation to save lives or selecting a burial site that brings the family together across generations?

c. **Unfulfilled Goals, Unresolved Conflicts, and Their Influence on One's Choices**

Addressing Regrets or Incomplete Journeys

- What personal goals have I never achieved, and how might the symbolism of certain rites—like planting a memorial tree or scattering ashes in a meaningful place—help me find peace with those unmet aspirations?
- What internal conflicts, such as feeling torn between tradition and personal conviction, can I acknowledge and resolve through the choices I make about how my body is laid to rest?

Reconciliation Through Symbolism

- How can choosing a particular method—such as donating my organs—serve as a final act of service or kindness, helping me reconcile regrets about not doing more for others in life?
- How might honoring cultural or religious rites heal old family tensions or provide a final, unifying gesture that mends strained relationships?

Transforming Loss into Legacy

- How can selecting a method of transition that reflects my values—such as sustainability, compassion, or faith—help transform feelings of unfinished business into a sense of legacy and forward-looking energy?
- How might the method of handling my body's remains serve as a quiet message of love or understanding to those who may have once misunderstood me?

d. **The Search for Meaning and Reconciliation: Spiritual Insights and Inner Peace**

Aligning with Spiritual Beliefs

- How do my religious, spiritual, or philosophical beliefs about the soul, the afterlife, or divine presence guide my choices for the body's final arrangements?
- What practice—such as cremation, burial in sacred ground, or rituals led by spiritual leaders—best reflects the core tenets of my faith or worldview?

Honoring Life's Impermanence

- How does acknowledging the impermanence of the physical form inspire me to choose a transition that symbolizes release, transformation, or return to the earth's embrace?
- How can I view these decisions as part of a sacred cycle—ashes returning to the cosmos, the body returning to the soil—as an affirmation of life's continuity?

Finding Inner Harmony and Purpose

- How will my choices help me reconcile my earthly existence with the mysteries of creation, reinforcing that my life and death hold meaning within a larger spiritual tapestry?
- How can confronting the reality of my body's transition help me find acceptance and peace, knowing that I've arranged a respectful and meaningful farewell?

Offering a Final Blessing

- How can I integrate prayers, blessings, or silent intentions into my final arrangements, transforming my body's departure into a final spiritual gift to myself and the world?
- How might envisioning my final bodily transition as a sacred act help me face mortality with courage, gratitude, and serenity?

By engaging with these questions, you can thoughtfully navigate the complex decisions surrounding the body's transition after death. Reflection upon personal memories, the impact on relationships, unresolved life elements, and spiritual convictions reveals a path that honors your entire life story. Balancing family needs, cultural traditions, and personal values, you can arrive at arrangements that feel authentic, compassionate, and spiritually resonant.

In doing so, these decisions become more than logistical choices; they emerge as profound gestures of identity, love, and faith. Through intentional planning, the final chapter of life can mirror its fullest truths—dignity, meaning, connection, and the sacred journey toward eternal peace.

Chapter 5. Practical and Logistical Preparations

5.1. **Advance Directives and Legal Documents**: Finalizing wills, living wills, powers of attorney, and medical directives.

Below is a list of reflective and introspective questions related to "Advance Directives and Legal Documents." These questions encourage you to look beyond the technicalities of wills, living wills, powers of attorney, and medical directives, and toward the emotional, spiritual, and relational dimensions of these preparations. By exploring personal memories, relationships, unfulfilled ambitions, and deeper meanings, you can bring authenticity, clarity, and peace to the process of finalizing these vital documents.

a. Personal Experiences and Memories: Drawing Guidance from One's Life Story

Learning from Past Challenges

- What previous life events—such as family disputes over inheritance, confusion about medical decisions, or difficulty accessing funds—inform my desire to be clear and fair in my own directives now?
- What memories of witnessing loved ones struggle without clear guidance in legal or medical matters at the end of life shape my own approach to planning and decision-making?

Aligning Documents with Core Values

- Which personal values—such as compassion, fairness, generosity, or self-sufficiency—do I most wish to reflect in my legal arrangements?
- When I look back on my life's defining moments, how do I want these legal documents to support the principles I've consistently tried to uphold?

Overcoming Emotional Hurdles

- What feelings of anxiety, fear, or reluctance do I need to acknowledge before I can confidently finalize these directives?
- How can recalling times when I responsibly managed other complex challenges remind me of my capability to approach end-of-life preparations with strength and wisdom?

b. Relationships and Interpersonal Connections: Nurturing Harmony Through Clear Guidance

Supporting Loved Ones After I'm Gone

- How might having a well-structured will and advance directives ease the emotional burdens on my loved ones, preventing disagreements or uncertainty?
- Which individuals—family members, close friends, spiritual advisors—should know the contents of my documents, and how can I present my decisions to them with clarity and kindness?

Fostering Open Communication

- What conversations do I need to have with potential healthcare proxies, executors, or financial power of attorney agents to ensure they understand and respect my wishes?
- How can I prepare to listen to my loved ones' concerns or fears about the directives I set, creating space for dialogue and reassurance?

Leaving a Legacy of Understanding

- How can finalizing these documents serve as a final gift of love, demonstrating that I cared enough to make complex decisions easier for those I leave behind?
- How might my legal and medical directives reinforce family unity, empathy, or forgiveness, offering a blueprint for peaceful resolution?

c. Unfulfilled Goals, Unresolved Conflicts, and Using Documents to Find Closure

Addressing Lingering Disputes

- How can making fair and transparent distributions of my assets help ease unresolved family conflicts, long-standing misunderstandings, or resentments?
- How might clarifying my wishes in legal documents bring a sense of justice, equality, or even reconciliation to strained relationships?

Redirecting Unfulfilled Ambitions

- What dreams do I regret not accomplishing, and how can directing portions of my estate or supporting certain causes through my will extend my values beyond my lifetime?
- How might designating charitable bequests or scholarships help transform feelings of "unfinished business" into a meaningful contribution to future generations?

Creating Spiritual and Emotional Bridges

- How can crafting medical directives and end-of-life care instructions bring me peace by ensuring that my care aligns with my moral and spiritual principles, even if I could not fully live them out earlier in my life?
- How might choosing a trusted individual to make healthcare decisions on my behalf represent a healing act, ensuring they understand my beliefs and honor them compassionately?

d. The Search for Meaning and Reconciliation: Spiritual Dimensions of Legal Preparations

Honoring Life's Sacredness

- How do my spiritual or religious beliefs about life's purpose, the afterlife, or the sanctity of the body inform how I arrange my legal and medical directives?
- How can I view this process not merely as paperwork, but as a final articulation of my moral compass, my relationship with the divine, and my legacy of faith?

Embracing Humility and Surrender

- How can preparing these documents become an act of acknowledging my mortality, embracing impermanence, and surrendering control to a greater spiritual reality?
- How does accepting this reality help free me from fear, allowing trust—whether in a higher power, the universe, or my loved ones—to guide my decisions?

Transforming Anxiety into Purpose

- How can the careful planning of legal directives become a spiritual exercise, transforming anxiety about death into a mindful and loving act of preparation and stewardship?
- In what ways does finalizing these directives help me come to terms with the full arc of my life, integrating successes and failures into a testament of inner growth and faith?

e. Integration and Conclusion: Emerging with Clarity, Peace, and Meaning

Achieving Authenticity in Legal Arrangements

- As I finalize my documents, how do I ensure that each decision—distribution of assets, healthcare directives, executor appointments—authentically reflects who I have been and who I aspire to be at life's end?
- How can I take pride in knowing that my careful planning reflects my integrity, consideration, and spiritual maturity?

Offering a Guiding Light for Others

- How might the process I undertake now serve as a model for younger family members or friends, inspiring them to approach their own mortality with courage and foresight?
- How can I find solace in knowing that my careful arrangements will not only ease the lives of my loved ones but also inspire them to honor their own values when their time comes?

Embracing the Path Ahead

- How can completing this process leave me with a calmer heart, knowing that I have aligned legalities with love and meaning, ensuring my final chapter is guided by thoughtfulness and grace?
- How can acknowledging my efforts as a sacred and compassionate act help me face the future—however long or short—with equanimity and hope?

By engaging with these questions, you can reframe the sometimes daunting task of preparing advance directives and legal documents into a profound spiritual and emotional journey. Instead of seeing it as a mere administrative hurdle, you can discover in this process a chance to unify your life's lessons, love, faith, and values into a coherent, compassionate legacy. This integration empowers you to approach the end of life with a sense of calm dignity, knowing they have prepared a roadmap that respects both earthly responsibilities and transcendent truths.

5.2. **Financial and Estate Planning**: Ensuring loved ones are financially secure, organizing finances, insurance, and assets.

Below is a set of reflective and introspective questions focused on "Financial and Estate Planning." These questions are designed to guide you in contemplating the emotional and spiritual dimensions of ensuring loved ones' financial security, organizing assets, and preparing insurance or estate documents. Organized into thematic categories, they encourage deep reflection on personal history, relationships, unmet aspirations, and the search for meaning. By engaging thoughtfully with these questions, you can infuse your financial and estate planning process with compassion, wisdom, and spiritual integrity.

a. **Personal Experiences and Memories: Learning from the Past**

Revisiting Financial Journeys

- Which financial decisions throughout my life—wise investments, charitable giving, costly mistakes—have taught me the most about responsibility, generosity, and stewardship?
- Have previous financial hardships or windfalls shaped my values regarding money and material security? How do these experiences inform my current planning?

Acknowledging Shifts in Perspective

- How has my attitude toward wealth and possessions evolved over time?
- How do I now view money less as a source of power or status and more as a means to support, nurture, and care for those who depend on me?

Reconciling Past Challenges

- What financial regrets—such as debts left unpaid, ill-considered loans, or missed savings opportunities—do I need to acknowledge and release as I prepare for the end of my life?
- How can recognizing my financial missteps help me find greater clarity, compassion, and moral guidance for my current estate planning decisions?

b. Relationships and Interpersonal Connections: Ensuring Care and Fairnes

Providing Security for Loved Ones

- As I consider distributing assets, how can I ensure that my loved ones feel supported and valued?
- How can I communicate my financial plans openly with family members to ensure they understand the reasoning behind my decisions and feel included rather than surprised or disappointed?

Balancing Needs and Fairness

- Who among my relatives or friends—such as children, elderly parents, or siblings facing hardship—are especially vulnerable, and how can my estate planning help alleviate their burdens?
- How might I strive for fairness, compassion, or equality, especially if family dynamics are complex?

Honoring Emotional Legacies

- Beyond money and property, what intangible gifts—life lessons, family traditions, moral guidance—how might my careful financial arrangements help preserve?
- How can I use the distribution of assets to encourage unity, reconciliation, or understanding among loved ones, reinforcing that relationships hold greater value than material wealth?

c. Unfulfilled Goals, Unresolved Conflicts, and Their Influence on Financial Choices

Redirecting Unmet Aspirations

- What dreams—such as educational projects, philanthropic endeavors, or creative works—did I never realize, and how can my financial planning now support those goals in my absence?
- How might directing funds toward a scholarship, charitable trust, or cultural initiative bring closure and meaning to aspirations I couldn't fulfill personally?

Healing Old Wounds Through Generosity

- How might unresolved resentments or conflicts be softened through an act of financial kindness, such as forgiving a debt or making an equal distribution to demonstrate respect and acknowledgment?
- How can my estate decisions serve as a form of healing or apology, symbolically repairing strained relationships or long-standing family rifts?

Accepting Limitations and Letting Go

- How can I find peace by using what I have now to provide stability for others, even if I never achieved certain financial milestones I had long hoped for?
- How might letting go of control over outcomes—recognizing that I cannot guarantee how recipients will use their inheritance—help me surrender with faith and grace?

d. The Search for Meaning and Reconciliation: Spiritual Dimensions of Financial Planning

Aligning Wealth with Core Values

- How do my religious or spiritual beliefs guide my understanding of material wealth? Is it a gift to be stewarded responsibly, a temptation, or an opportunity to reflect divine generosity?
- How can I integrate my spiritual convictions into my estate plans by directing funds to charities that reflect my moral principles or ensuring long-term support for communities I care about?

Embracing the Transience of Material Things

- How does recognizing the impermanence of life affect my perspective on money, possessions, and property?
- In what ways can my planning reflect an understanding that true security lies not in accumulations, but in love, faith, and the eternal aspects of human existence?

Spiritual Growth Through Letting Go

- How can the process of clarifying my finances become an act of spiritual surrender, freeing me from attachments and allowing me to pass on blessings with an open heart?
- How might this process deepen my trust in something greater than wealth—be it community, divine guidance, or the resilience and resourcefulness of my loved ones?

e. Integration and Wholeness: Merging Practicality with Heartfelt Intent

Creating a Coherent Financial Legacy

- How does my estate plan articulate the story of my values, ensuring that those who inherit understand not just what I gave, but why I gave it?
- How have I documented my reasons for certain allocations—perhaps through letters or ethical wills—so that recipients can understand the deeper significance of their inheritance?

Engaging in Honest Reflection and Communication

- How can I remain prepared to revisit and revise my plans as new insights arise, ensuring that my arrangements stay aligned with my evolving spiritual understanding?
- What steps can I take to gather the courage to openly share my decisions and the spiritual meanings behind them with my loved ones, fostering transparency and reducing future uncertainties?

Emerging with Peace and Resolve

- How does reflecting on these questions help me feel more at peace, knowing I have done what I can to provide security, express love, and extend my values into the future?
- How can I rest in the awareness that my financial and estate planning has become a spiritual act, transcending mere transactions and serving as a final gesture of care, wisdom, and faith?

By engaging deeply with these questions, you can transform the often-daunting task of financial and estate planning into an opportunity for spiritual maturation and emotional healing. Rather than being solely administrative work, this process can serve as a final, loving conversation—a legacy that speaks from the heart, nurtures relationships, and reflects the essence of a life thoughtfully lived.

5.3. **Funeral and Memorial Service Arrangements**: Planning services that reflect personal values, cultural traditions, or desired atmosphere.

Below is a list of reflective and introspective questions related to "Funeral and Memorial Service Arrangements." These questions invite you to consider how you might design ceremonies that honor your personal values, cultural roots, spiritual beliefs, and emotional truths. Organized into thematic subcategories, the questions encourage a thoughtful, heartfelt approach that transcends mere logistics. By engaging with these prompts, you can shape end-of-life services that resonate deeply with your unique life story, relationships, and spiritual journey.

a. **Personal Experiences and Memories: Drawing Inspiration from Life's Journey**

Recalling Past Ceremonies and Traditions

- Which funerals, memorials, or cultural rites have I attended in the past that left a lasting impression on me?
- What elements—music, readings, personal stories, symbolic gestures—resonated most and why?
- What childhood memories of sacred rituals, family gatherings, or seasonal festivities could I incorporate to evoke warmth and continuity?

Highlighting Meaningful Symbols and Spaces

- What particular symbols—such as flowers, candles, art, or natural elements—reflect my personality, beliefs, or cherished values?
- Which locations—gardens, places of worship, family homes, community halls—feel most meaningful for my final farewell?

Capturing the Essence of a Life Story

- How can the memorial setting and chosen rituals reflect the key themes of my life—love of music, affinity for nature, commitment to service, dedication to family, or devotion to faith?
- What objects or artifacts—such as photographs, letters, or heirlooms— highlight pivotal moments, accomplishments, or lessons I have learned?

b. **Relationships and Interpersonal Connections: Honoring Bonds and Fostering Unity**

Involving Loved Ones and Community

- How do I imagine family, friends, neighbors, or spiritual mentors participating in the ceremony, and what roles might they play?
- How can I invite attendees to share their memories or blessings, perhaps through an open microphone, a memory table, or written tributes?

Bridging Cultural and Generational Gaps

- If my family or community is culturally or religiously diverse, how can I ensure the service includes elements that honor all backgrounds?
- How can I incorporate multilingual readings, music from various traditions, or representatives from different faiths to reflect the pluralism that shaped my life?

Fostering Reconciliation and Healing

- How can the memorial gently address strained relationships or unresolved tensions by fostering forgiveness, understanding, or shared prayer?
- How might the tone and content of the service bring peace, healing, or comfort to those I leave behind, reminding them of love's enduring strength?

c.   Unfulfilled Goals, Unresolved Conflicts, and Finding Closure through Ritual

Symbolizing Completion and Letting Go

- What ambitions or dreams did I never realize, and how might an aspect of the service—such as dedicating a song or poem—symbolically acknowledge these aspirations?
- How could including certain rituals—like lighting candles, planting a tree, or offering a silent moment—represent the release of regrets or the acceptance of life's natural limits?

Transforming Conflict into Wisdom

- How can I incorporate readings or prayers that reflect the lessons learned from areas of personal struggle or moral dilemmas I faced?
- How might focusing on hope, resilience, or compassion in the service help transcend past conflicts, demonstrating growth and understanding?

Honoring Imperfect Journeys

- How can I embrace the idea that life is inherently incomplete and frame the memorial to emphasize the beauty of striving, learning, and evolving rather than perfection?
- How might the service acknowledge not just successes, but also the honest imperfections, doubts, and questions that defined my human experience?

d. The Search for Meaning and Reconciliation: Spiritual Depth and Transcendence

Expressing Faith and Spiritual Beliefs

- How can I incorporate prayers, sacred texts, meditative moments, or spiritual music that authentically represent my spiritual outlook?
- What central spiritual theme—such as divine love, everlasting life, cosmic unity, reincarnation, or peace beyond understanding—do I want my memorial to convey?

Inviting Mystical Presence and Hope

- What elements—such as a candle that remains lit, a prayer for future generations, or a symbol of rebirth—can I include to suggest continuity beyond death and inspire hope among attendees?
- What rituals or words might reassure loved ones that, even though my physical presence is gone, my spirit endures in their hearts, memories, or spiritual realms?

Cultivating a Sacred Atmosphere

- How can I ensure the ceremony's atmosphere—through lighting, music, silence, or scripture—encourages calm reflection, sacred awe, and emotional warmth?
- How might I use nature's presence—such as open sky, water, or greenery—or religious symbols like crosses, mandalas, or icons to evoke a sense of divine mystery and gentle transcendence?

e. Integration: Weaving Together Practicality, Authenticity, and Love

Balancing Tradition and Innovation

- How can I blend traditional customs with modern expressions to craft a service that feels both rooted and evolving, honoring my past while acknowledging new dimensions of spiritual growth?

Clarity and Communication

- How can I ensure my wishes are clearly articulated and documented so that those who plan the memorial understand my intentions and can carry them out faithfully?

Leaving a Final Message of Love and Guidance

- What personal note, ethical will, or farewell message can I share to offer gratitude, blessings, or hope for my loved ones' futures?
- How do I want those attending my memorial to feel when they leave—uplifted, comforted, motivated to live with more kindness, faith, or purpose?

By contemplating these questions, you can guide yourself toward a funeral or memorial service arrangement that authentically mirrors your inner landscape. This reflective process transforms planning from a purely logistical task into a meaningful spiritual endeavor—one that helps ensure the final farewell is a testament to a life well-examined, relationships cherished, conflicts transcended, and faith affirmed.

5.4. **Digital Legacy and Communications**: Managing email accounts, social media profiles, and digital assets, leaving clear instructions.

Below is a set of introspective questions focused on "Digital Legacy and Communications." These questions invite you to think deeply about how your online presence—email accounts, social media profiles, digital assets—can be managed and passed on with intention and grace. Each category encourages reflection on personal history, relationships, unresolved matters, and spiritual meaning, ensuring that the process of shaping your digital legacy resonates with the soul's journey and the universal human experience of facing mortality.

a. **Personal Experiences and Memories: Understanding the Story Your Digital Footprint Tells**

Evaluating Your Digital Presence

- Which aspects of my online life—social media posts, blogs, photographs, creative projects—best reflect who I have become over the years?
- What are there digital spaces where I can consistently expressed my values, beliefs, or passions, and how might preserving them help tell my life's story?

Honoring Life's Milestones and Accomplishments

- Have I used digital platforms to celebrate personal milestones, share successes, or document meaningful moments? How do I want these reflections preserved or passed on?
- What old email correspondences or digital journals capture significant transformations, epiphanies, or lessons I've learned, and how might they remain accessible as part of my legacy?

Curating a Legacy of Memories

- What cherished digital photographs, videos, or voice recordings do I want to ensure are saved and easily found by loved ones?
- How comfortable am I with allowing future generations to browse my online presence—social media timelines or personal websites—to discover my personal evolution and growth?

b. **Relationships and Interpersonal Connections: Nurturing Bonds Beyond the Physical World**

Communicating Intentions to Loved Ones

- Who among my family and friends should have access to my digital accounts, and how can I guide them so that they understand my intentions for archiving, deleting, or sharing content?
- Who are the trusted individuals I can designate as digital "guardians" to ensure that meaningful online conversations, emails, or group chats are handled with respect and discretion?

Preserving Supportive Communities

- Have I formed online communities—faith-based discussion groups, forums for shared interests, or mentorship circles—that have played a nurturing role in my life, and how should I pass their stewardship on?
- How can I designate someone to share a final message of gratitude or farewell in online spaces, providing closure and comfort to those who have journeyed with me virtually?

Leaving Messages of Love and Guidance

- What steps can I take to leave behind scheduled messages, emails, or digital letters to loved ones, offering encouragement, blessings, or spiritual reflections after I'm gone?
- How might carefully chosen digital content—music playlists, inspirational quotes, saved articles—act as a final offering of wisdom or solace to those I leave behind?

c. **Unfulfilled Goals, Unresolved Conflicts, and Finding Peace through Digital Footprints**

Addressing Unfinished Digital Projects

- What creative or personal projects—such as unpublished writings, incomplete photo albums, or unfinished podcasts—living online would I like to see completed, shared, or peacefully brought to an end?
- How can I leave instructions for trusted individuals to finalize these projects, or would I prefer to let them remain private as an honest acceptance of life's unfinished business?

Releasing Digital Clutter and Conflicts

- What online content—such as old arguments, controversial posts, or regretful messages—no longer represents who I am or want to be remembered as, and how can I address these as an act of forgiveness and reconciliation?
- How might curating or deleting certain digital traces serve as a symbolic way of letting go of past misunderstandings or tensions, leaving a cleaner slate for my memory?

Transforming Regrets into Gifts

- If I feel remorse over certain online interactions—hurtful words or broken connections—what apologies, clarifications, or reconciliatory notes can I include in my digital legacy instructions?
- How might these thoughtful gestures help loved ones see my personal journey toward understanding, empathy, and humility, even after my death?

d. **The Search for Meaning and Reconciliation: Infusing Spiritual Depth into Your Digital Legacy**

Aligning Digital Presence with Spiritual Values

- How do my spiritual or religious beliefs inform the way I want my online identity to endure or fade away? Is my goal to reflect impermanence, celebrate eternal truth, or simply preserve cherished memories?
- How can I integrate faith-based readings, prayers, or blessings into my digital legacy to offer future generations a window into my spiritual worldview?

Embracing Impermanence and Transformation

- In a medium designed to preserve information indefinitely, how do I balance the human need for closure, acceptance, and the understanding that physical life is finite?

- How might choosing to close certain accounts or delete content reflect my belief in letting go, moving on, or embracing the spiritual mystery beyond human existence?

Creating a Sacred Digital Space

- How can I view careful arrangement of my digital estate—selecting what to share, what to protect, what to delete—as a sacred act, a spiritual ritual of leaving my earthly narrative in order?
- In embracing this curation as a spiritual practice, how do I find comfort in the idea that I am blessing the digital paths I leave behind, turning them into gentle reminders of faith, love, and hope?

e. **Integration and Preparation: Formulating a Clear and Purposeful Plan**

Transparency and Clarity in Instructions

- What written guidelines or designated digital estate executors have I prepared to manage my accounts, passwords, and digital permissions?
- How can I ensure these instructions are both explicit and compassionate, guiding loved ones to carry out my wishes without confusion or added stress?

Sharing the Meaning Behind My Choices

- How can I explain the reasons behind my digital legacy decisions—why certain accounts are deleted or specific memories saved—so loved ones understand their spiritual or emotional significance?
- What might I include in a personal note or "digital legacy letter" to offer context, gratitude, and guidance, helping those who follow my plan see it as part of my final act of love and care?

Emerging with Peace and Authenticity

- How does reflecting on these questions bring me peace, knowing I have approached my digital legacy with integrity, empathy, and reverence?
- How does the clarity of my instructions and the intentionality behind my digital curation allow me to face the future with calm, knowing my values and memories will be handled lovingly after my death?

By contemplating these questions, you can transform the often-overlooked task of managing digital assets into a meaningful, soul-enriching endeavor. It becomes not merely a matter of passwords and permissions, but a profound opportunity to shape your virtual footprint into a legacy that honors your life's story, nurtures relationships, reflects their spiritual beliefs, and offers enduring guidance and comfort to those who remain.

5.5. **Leaving Written or Recorded Messages**: Offering guidance, advice, or comfort in letters, video recordings, or journals for future generations.

Below is a set of reflective and introspective questions related to "Leaving Written or Recorded Messages." These questions help you consider the wisdom, comfort, and guidance you might want to convey to loved ones and future generations. Each category encourages deep self-exploration, linking personal memories, relationships, lingering regrets, spiritual insights, and the search for meaning. By engaging sincerely with these prompts, you can create a final offering that honors your life's journey, nurtures healing, and inspires hope.

a. **Personal Experiences and Memories: Drawing on a Life Well-Lived**

Recalling Pivotal Moments

- What stories from my life capture the essence of who I am and what I value most?
- What specific life lessons, drawn from moments of adversity, triumph, or quiet perseverance, do I wish to pass on to others?

Highlighting Cultural and Family Traditions

- Which family rituals, cultural celebrations, or spiritual observances have shaped my identity, and how can I articulate their significance for future generations?
- How can I share recipes, songs, prayers, or proverbs that hold special meaning, creating a tangible link to our heritage?

Reflecting on Personal Growth

- In what ways have I changed over the years—becoming more compassionate, more patient, or more forgiving—and what sparked these transformations?
- What hard-won wisdom can I convey about facing fears, embracing uncertainty, and remaining open to life's unfolding mysteries?

b. **Relationships and Interpersonal Connections: Offering Love, Forgiveness, and Encouragement**

Expressing Appreciation and Love

- To whom do I owe gratitude—mentors, friends, family members, community leaders—and how can I acknowledge their impact on my life's path?
- How might heartfelt messages of love, admiration, or pride reinforce the bonds that continue beyond my physical presence?

Encouraging Understanding and Compassion

- What instances in my life, where understanding another's pain or perspective changed how I related to them, can I share to encourage future generations to approach relationships with empathy?
- What guidance can I give about navigating conflicts, setting healthy boundaries, or extending kindness, even when it's difficult?

Affirming the Power of Connection

- How can I emphasize the importance of community, cooperation, and mutual support, so that those who read or hear my words feel inspired to nurture their own relationships?
- What do I wish to say that reassures loved ones they are never truly alone, and that human warmth and solidarity endure even in challenging times?

c. **Unfulfilled Goals, Unresolved Conflicts, and Finding Peace through Honest Communication**

Acknowledging Unfinished Business

- What personal ambitions did I not realize, and how can sharing these candid reflections help future generations find acceptance and resilience in facing their own unmet goals?
- How can I highlight the importance of valuing the journey itself—learning from missteps, cherishing small joys, and recognizing that life's meaning doesn't hinge solely on achievements?

Mending Emotional Wounds

- What regrets—such as missed apologies, unspoken words of love, or withheld forgiveness—can I now address directly in my messages?
- How can open and vulnerable admissions of mistakes or misunderstandings encourage healing and show that embracing vulnerability can lead to deeper love and respect?

Inspiring Forgiveness and Reconciliation

- How can I model the process of forgiveness—both for myself and others—by acknowledging past hurts and affirming that compassion can heal old wounds?

- How might my honesty and willingness to confront unresolved conflicts encourage future generations to approach their own challenges with courage and grace?

d. The Search for Meaning and Reconciliation: Weaving Spiritual Insights into Guidance

Articulating Core Beliefs and Values

- What spiritual truths, faith traditions, or philosophical concepts guided my moral compass, and how can I explain their relevance to those who may walk their own path of belief or doubt?
- What core values—such as integrity, generosity, humility, or reverence for life—do I hope my descendants will carry forward, and how can I distill these into a lasting message?

Embracing Mystery and Impermanence

- How can I help future generations understand that uncertainty and impermanence are inherent to the human experience, urging them to find meaning within life's transient beauty?
- In what ways can I encourage seeking the divine or finding sacredness in everyday life, reminding them that spirituality often emerges in ordinary moments of gratitude, compassion, or awe?

Offering Hope and Direction

- What words can I share that inspire hope, guiding others to look beyond struggle and darkness toward growth, learning, and redemption?
- How can I offer reassurance that their lives—like mine—are part of a larger narrative, encouraging them to find purpose, serve others, and cherish each moment?

e. Integrating Practicality with Profound Intention: Ensuring Clarity and Accessibility

Choosing the Right Medium and Tone

- Which medium—letters, video recordings, audio messages, or handwritten journals—best conveys my authenticity, warmth, and sincerity?
- What tone—plain, poetic, humorous, or prayerful—reflects who I am and how I wish to be remembered?

Guiding Future Use of the Messages

- How can I provide instructions for when and how loved ones should access these messages—during personal milestones, family gatherings, times of grief, or moments of doubt—so they serve as timely beacons of support?
- How might I ensure that my voice remains a gentle presence, not an imposing directive, allowing future generations the freedom to interpret and integrate my guidance as they choose?

Releasing the Messages with Peace and Trust

- As I finalize these communications, how can I let go of the outcome, trusting that those who receive my words will glean from them what they need in their own time and way?
- How does creating these messages bring me a sense of peace, knowing they bridge past, present, and future, weaving my voice into the tapestry of family heritage, collective memory, and spiritual continuity?

By contemplating these questions, you can approach the creation of letters, recordings, or journals with clarity and depth. This reflective process transforms the act of leaving messages into a sacred exchange—a gift that conveys personal truths, fosters enduring love, heals lingering hurts, and illuminates spiritual insights for generations yet to come. Through these thoughtful offerings, your legacy transcends the boundaries of time, accompanying loved ones as a guiding presence, a whisper of wisdom, and a reminder that love and understanding endure.